The Easy Gourmet

Entertaining Made Fun and Simple

SAFEWAY

Canada Safeway Limited 🍁

EILEEN DWILLIES
ANN MERLING
ANGELA NILSEN
EDENA SHELDON

OPUS PRODUCTIONS INC.
VANCOUVER

Published and produced for Canada Safeway Limited by
Opus Productions Inc.
1128 Homer Street
Vancouver, B.C., Canada
V6B 2X6

© Copyright 1989 Opus Productions Inc.

Recipes © Copyright 1989 Eileen Dwillies, Ann Merling,
   Angela Nilsen, Edena Sheldon

Photography © Copyright 1989 Derik Murray

Canadian Cataloguing in Publication Data
   Main entry under title:
   Entertaining made fun and simple

              (The Easy Gourmet ; v.4)
              Includes index.
              ISBN 0-921926-03-0

   1. Entertaining. 2. Cookery. 3. Menus. I. Series.
   TX731.E58 1989   641.5'68   C89-091527-X

Corporate Consultant: Mark McCurdy, Palmer Jarvis Advertising
Editor: Mary Schendlinger
Production Manager: Orest Kinasevych
Designers: Tim Kelly, David Counsell
Recipe Coordinator: Eileen Dwillies
Food Stylist: Eileen Dwillies
Test Kitchen Manager and Food Stylist Assistant: Arline Smith
Test Kitchen Staff: Kathy Alexander, Margot Brown, Louisa Capostinsky, Fran Donis,
              Betsy Filion, Judy Lye, Jeannie Meier, Jennie Meier, Joyce Miller,
              Marge Milne, Alison Sclater, Arline Smith

Produced exclusively on the IBM Personal Publishing System and
IBM PS/2 Personal Systems.

On the cover: Fried Polenta (p. 111).

Printed in Canada by Friesen Printers.

"The Easy Gourmet" TM

TABLE OF CONTENTS

About the authors

Eileen Dwillies, whose recipes and articles have been published in *Western Living, Canadian Living* and other Canadian periodicals, also works as a food stylist for print and television, and teaches cooking in her home. Ann Merling is a microwave consultant, teacher and home economist whose extensive experience includes twelve years working with microwave manufacturers and teaching microwave cooking to consumers. Angela Nilsen, a home economist, food stylist and cooking instructor, has written numerous recipes and articles for publications in Europe and North America, and was a food writer with the *Vancouver Sun* for seven years. Edena Sheldon's food features and recipes have appeared for U.S. magazines, newspapers and cookbooks including *Bon Appétit, Sunset* and the *Los Angeles Times*. More recently, her work has been published in Canada, in the *Canada Cooks!* series and in *Western Living Magazine*. She enjoys a continuing reputation as a food and prop stylist.

All four authors bring to the recipes their extensive food writing experience, the unique influences of their world travels, and most of all their appreciation of the cooking traditions of Western Canada, where all of them make their home.

About the recipes

Every recipe in this book is carefully and thoroughly kitchen-tested, by a team that includes both new and experienced cooks.

For convenience in shopping and measuring, we "rounded off" in listing the metric quantities of recipe ingredients: 1 lb. is converted as 500 g, rather than the technically correct 454 g; 1/2 lb. is shown as 250 g, and so on.

All of the microwave recipes were tested in microwave ovens of 700 watts, so if yours is in the 600 watt range, add 15% to the suggested cooking times. And remember to start with the minimum suggested time and add extra if necessary—every microwave, like every convection oven, is unique.

We used large eggs and whole milk unless specified otherwise, and we used unsalted butter without exception. When you cook with herbs, remember that dried herbs are much more concentrated than fresh ones, so if you substitute dried herbs for fresh, use one-third the amount. When a recipe calls for wine, liqueur, or other alcoholic beverage, there is usually a substitute ingredient listed. There are non-alcoholic cooking wines and liqueurs available, but unless the recipe specifically calls for them, we did not use them, as their salt content is quite high.

INTRODUCTION

Welcome to *The Easy Gourmet: Entertaining Made Fun and Simple*, the fourth in a unique series of cookbooks created to celebrate Canada Safeway's Sixtieth Anniversary.

Entertaining can be as simple as a friend dropping in for a visit or as elaborate as a holiday gathering for a crowd. Whatever the occasion, entertaining guests means offering food and beverages—an age-old expression of welcome. Specially designed for both casual and festive get-togethers, this book is a rich selection of recipes and menu suggestions that can be adapted to your own special events. It was created by the four talented food writers who created Volume One, *Entrées: The Main Event*; Volume Two, *Summer Salads and Barbecue Cookouts*; and Volume Three, *Hearty Winter Stews & Casseroles*.

Some of the recipes in this volume, as in all of the books in the series, are designed for preparation in the microwave. Look for the special microwave symbol ▥

The Menus

To reflect the great variety of occasions that call for special foods, the book is divided into four main sections: Brunches, Casual Appetizers, Dinners, and Late Evening. Every kind of menu is to be found in these pages. Some are designed for nibbling (the Greek Appetizer Party—simple but exotic hors d'oeuvres for a group of friends) and others are veritable feasts (the Traditional Christmas Dinner). Some menus, such as the Celebration Dinner for Two, suit intimate get-togethers, while others, like the Autumn Bonfire Party, are designed for exuberant crowds. Light meals are to be found here (the Sunrise Special, needing only a good Sunday paper for ambience), as well as more hearty fare like the down-home Harvest Farm Brunch. There's something for all ages: the Children's Pizza Party is the start of a great birthday gathering, the Rock'n'Roll Buffet is the ideal ice-breaker for the young adult set, and the Sports Fans All-Out Brunch or Candlelight Feast will delight the grown-ups. In appreciation of international tastes and styles, menus like the Mexican Fiesta, Spicy Curry Dinner, and New Wave Italian Dinner boast up-to-date exotic recipes that look as good as they taste. The book also includes gatherings that focus on scrumptious desserts—the recipes in the After-Theatre Dessert Party or Chocolate Lovers' Delight are good reasons to throw a great party.

All of the menus have been assembled for the variety of tastes, colours, and textures that work well together when guests are expected. The authors also provide special tips on creating an enjoyable atmosphere for that special occasion: watch for notes on seasonal colours, table linens, serving dishes, and garnishes. But think of the menus as ideas and suggestions, collected to inspire you as you get ready for your next special event. If a particular recipe catches your eye, go ahead and try it! Spicy Honey-Glazed Prawns are every bit as good in a light family supper in front of the TV as they are in the

Centre-Ice Pub Party, and the Swiss Chocolate Fondue is a smash hit at a high school graduation party as well as in the suggested Midnight Fondue menu. This book is fun to read as well as being a superb collection of delicious, kitchen-tested recipes, so page through it, imagine your own party, and mix and match to your heart's content.

The Recipes

Half the fun of a special occasion is the special foods that go with it. These recipes are memorably tasty and impressive to present—but they are also versatile. Simple enough to serve on even an ordinary day, the dishes are prepared with ingredients that are familiar, economical, and easy to find. Thanks to modern storage and transportation methods, Safeway's wide selection of fresh meat, seafood, produce, and other ingredients are readily available and reliably high-quality.

Some of the recipes are comfortably traditional: Turkey with All the Trimmings, Potted Cheddar, and classic Scottish Dundee Cake will never go out of style! Others have been created for your more adventurous moments: try the ultra-contemporary Asparagus Flan with Maltaise Sauce or Savoury Mousse with Three Caviars. In this volume you will find sparkling new additions to your favourite "company" dishes, and ideas that are sure to start new holiday traditions for your family.

Great Entertaining

Today's cooks lead full and busy lives. More than ever before, taking the time to prepare gorgeous and delicious food for family and friends is a gesture of loving generosity. But the host and hostess deserve to have as much fun as their guests, so the recipes and menus offered in this book express the new style of entertaining: fresh, simple, elegant foods, presented beautifully but informally, so that you can relax and enjoy the company of those special people. Observe these few tips on entertaining, and have yourself a great time.

Planning the Food
Choose the menu for your event. Start with the menus suggested here, and add the foods and beverages of your choice, keeping in mind the number of guests and the type of occasion. Now read the recipes carefully, and make sure you have all the ingredients you need—even the always-in-the-cupboard ingredients such as flour, onions, and icing sugar. Then check to see that you have party go-withs like cream for the coffee and ice for the punch.

Planning the Presentation
Picture the table, and gather what you need for serving and presenting the food: the centrepiece, serving bowls and platters, dishes, cutlery, and linens. Think about the placement of chairs and how your guests will be served. Does that silver tray need polishing, and is there a cloth for the small side table that will hold the tea service? The more you plan in advance, the more smoothly your party will go.

Cooking Ahead of Time

Many of these recipes can be made ahead completely or partially, with just a quick last-minute heat-up in the oven, skillet, or microwave, and a fast and fabulous garnish. The menus also take full advantage of the delicious array of convenience foods available in Safeway's grocery, deli, and bakery departments. As you plan your event, take note of the preparation time for each recipe. Do as much as you can ahead of time, and plan the finishing touches so that everything is ready at once.

Welcoming Your Guests

The secret of great entertaining is making your guests comfortable, and the best way to do this is to be comfortable yourself. If you plan ahead and cook ahead, you'll be much more relaxed when your guests arrive. In all stages of that planning, think about comfort and convenience first. If you are serving finger foods, make sure they are small enough to handle and not dripping with sauce—unless, of course, the gathering is very informal and guests are expected to lick their fingers! For buffets, arrange the table so people can move freely as they fill their plates. The dishes and cutlery go at one end, followed by conveniently-placed bowls and platters of food with appropriate serving utensils. Beverages are best placed on a small table off to the side, as are desserts, coffee, and tea. Full-course meals and casual fork-and-knife fare call for a sit-down arrangement. Allow each guest plenty of room and arrange seating in a circle or square to encourage conversation. In serving any kind of meal or appetizer, never skimp on linens!

And remember, you don't need expensive accompaniments or fancy dishes and linens to present the foods in this book to their full advantage. Invite people who enjoy each other's company, and create the right atmosphere with simple flourishes. A basket of fresh flowers at a brunch, a few shimmering candles at dinner or a late-night gathering, wooden bowls and cutting boards for a rustic touch, cloth napkins for a whisper of luxury...these and your affection for those special people, along with the mouth-watering and attractive dishes to be found in this book, are the real secrets to simply great entertaining.

BRUNCHES

Nothing starts a special day like a very special brunch. Celebrate a leisurely autumn Sunday with the Harvest Farm Brunch, or plan a Country French Omelette Party for a touch of elegance, or serve up a Lovers' Brunch just for you and your sweetheart. The menus and recipes in this section are worth getting up for!

SPORTS FANS ALL-OUT BRUNCH

When autumn rolls around, there's no better time for a gang of sports fanatics to gather 'round the big screen, cheer on the day's favourite, and nibble on lots of good mid-day munchies: spicy, savoury, some dips, some things hot and crispy—all bursting with south-of-the-border flavour. Serves 8-10.

Guacamole Olé　　　　　　　*Tostada chips*
Chile Con Queso Dip　　　　*Platter of chilled raw vegetables*
Spicy Southwest Chicken
　Wings
Tiny Empanadas
Cinnamon-Sugar Sopapillas

GUACAMOLE OLÉ

Avocado is high on everyone's list of favourites, and is sure to stay there when your guests taste this wonderful chunky guacamole, flavoured with chili and cilantro. Serve in a big bowl surrounded by crisp tostada chips. Makes 3 cups (750 mL).

4	large, ripe avocados	4
1/2 tsp.	salt	2 mL
2 tbsp.	fresh lime or lemon juice	30 mL
2	small cloves garlic, pressed	2
1	firm, ripe tomato, halved, seeded, and diced	1
1	4 oz. (114 g) can diced roasted chiles	1
4 tbsp.	minced fresh cilantro	60 ml
1/2 tsp.	chili powder	2 mL
	bottled hot pepper sauce to taste	

Halve each avocado, discard the pit, and scoop out the flesh. Mash to a coarse purée with the back of a fork. Add the remaining ingredients. Taste and correct for seasonings. Cover with plastic wrap, and refrigerate up to 4 hours. Serve chilled.

CHILI CON QUESO DIP

Silky smooth with a bite of chili, this dip is addictively delicious. Serve it with tostada chips and a big platter of crisp raw vegetables. Colourful, nutritious, and very, very tasty! Makes 2 1/2 cups (625 mL).

2 tbsp.	corn oil	30 mL
2 cups	minced onion	500 mL
1/4 tsp.	chili powder	1 mL
1	4 oz. (114 g) can diced roasted chiles	1
1	5 1/2 oz. (160 mL) can evaporated milk	1
12 oz.	shredded Monterey jack cheese	375 g
	salt and pepper to taste	
	chili powder to taste	

Heat the oil in a heavy saucepan over medium heat. Add the minced onion and sauté 1-2 minutes. Stir in the 1/4 tsp. (1 mL) chili powder and roasted chiles and saute 1-2 minutes. Stir in the evaporated milk, bring to a simmer, and cook until slightly thickened and creamy, about 5 minutes. Over barely warm heat, add the shredded cheese in small amounts, and stir after each addition just until the cheese is melted. Season to taste with salt and pepper, sprinkle with a pinch of chili powder, and serve warm in a pretty crockery bowl.

SPICY SOUTHWEST CHICKEN WINGS

These tangy, succulent chicken wings may be marinated 24 hours ahead of time, and baked several hours before guests arrive. Serve at room temperature, or quickly reheat in a 300°F (150°C) oven 10 minutes before serving.

4 lbs.	chicken wings, separated in half,	2 kg
	wing tips discarded (or chicken drumettes)	
1/3 cup	corn oil	75 mL
1/2 cup	finely minced onion	125 mL
4	cloves garlic, pressed	4
1	10 oz. (250 mL) jar lime or lemon marmalade	1
1/2 cup	cider vinegar	125 mL
4 tbsp.	fresh lime juice	60 mL
	grated rind of 2 limes (green part only)	
1/2 cup	finely minced fresh cilantro	125 mL
2 tsp.	bottled hot pepper sauce	10 mL
2 tbsp.	brown sugar	30 mL
1/4 tsp.	*each* ground cloves and chili powder	1 mL
1 tsp.	ground paprika	5 mL
	fresh lime wedges and sprigs of cilantro for garnish	

Rinse the chicken wings with cold water, drain, and pat dry. Set aside. In a saucepan, heat the oil over medium-high heat. Add the onion and garlic and sauté until softened and pale golden. Add the marmalade, vinegar, lime juice, lime peel, cilantro, hot pepper sauce, brown sugar, cloves, chili powder and paprika. Bring to a simmer, stirring, until the marmalade is melted and all ingredients are blended. Simmer, uncovered, 15-20 minutes until bubbly and slightly thickened. Remove from the heat and set aside to cool to room temperature.

Pour the cooled sauce over the chicken wings in a shallow glass baking dish, toss to coat evenly, and cover. Marinate overnight.

Heat the oven to 375°F (190°C). Place the marinated wings, skin side down, on a large shallow baking pan. Bake 15 minutes. Meanwhile, pour the reserved marinade into a saucepan and bring to a boil. Cook until syrupy and thickened. Turn the wings skin side up. Brush the marinade over the wings and bake 15-20 minutes longer, or until tender and rich golden brown.

Heat the broiler. Broil the wings 6 inches (15 cm) from the heat 4-5 minutes until slightly charred and crispy brown. Remove and cool 25 minutes.

Serve the wings mounded on a large platter, surrounded by lime wedges and garnished with sprigs of cilantro.

TINY EMPANADAS

Empanadas are pastry turnovers found all over Latin America and prepared with a variety of fillings. This version, with flavoured chunky beef, can be baked up to 1 week in advance, wrapped tightly, and frozen. Reheat them in a 400°F (200°C) oven for about 8 minutes before serving. Makes 4 dozen appetizers, each 3 1/2 inches (8.5 cm) in diameter.

1 lb.	lean ground beef	500 g
1	onion, minced	1
2	cloves garlic, pressed	2
1/2 cup	raisins or dried currants	125 mL
1 tsp.	ground cinnamon	5 mL
1/4 tsp.	*each* ground cumin, cloves, and coriander	1 mL
2 tsp.	chili powder	10 mL
2 tbsp.	brown sugar	30 mL
1 tbsp.	cider vinegar	15 mL
4 tbsp.	tomato-based chili sauce	60 mL
1 tsp.	salt	5 mL
	freshly ground black pepper to taste	
1/2 cup	sliced, pitted ripe black olives	125 mL
2	14 oz. (400 g) pkgs. frozen pie pastry, thawed	2

For the filling, fry the ground beef in a skillet over medium-high heat. Break up the meat to crumble, and add the onion and garlic. Sauté, stirring, until the meat is no longer pink and the onion is pale golden. Add the raisins, cinnamon, cumin, cloves, coriander, chili powder, brown sugar, vinegar, chili sauce, and salt. Season liberally with pepper and stir in the olives. Heat until bubbly and glossy, about 10 minutes. Set aside to cool completely.

For the turnovers, roll the thawed pastry out onto a floured surface, 1/8 inch (6 mm) thick. With a biscuit cutter, cut out 3 1/2 inch (8.5 cm) rounds.

Heat the oven to 400°F (200°C). Place a rounded teaspoonful of the filling on each half. Fold the pastry over to close, moistening the edges with a bit of cold water to seal. Press the edges together all around with a fork. Place the turnovers on an ungreased baking sheet, 1 inch (2.5 cm) apart.

Prick the top of each turnover once with the tines of a fork. Bake 20-25 minutes, or until golden brown. Serve hot or warm.

CINNAMON-SUGAR SOPAPILLAS

Serve these puffy, fried, cloud-like pillows with a dusting of cinnamon-sugar for dessert. Accompany them with your favourite hot chocolate, flavoured with a bit of cinnamon and topped with whipped cream.

	corn or vegetable oil for frying	
3	7 1/2 oz. (215 g) tubes refrigerated buttermilk biscuits	3
1 cup	sugar	250 mL
4 tbsp.	ground cinnamon	60 mL

Pour the oil to a depth of 3 inches (7.5 cm) into a heavy, deep skillet. Heat to 375°F (190°C). (The frying temperature is right when a bit of bread dropped in rises to the top immediately and begins to sizzle.) With floured scissors, snip each separated ready-to-bake biscuit in half. Drop the halves into the hot oil several at a time (do not crowd) and fry on both sides until puffed and golden brown. Remove with a slotted spoon and drain on absorbent paper. Combine the sugar and cinnamon. While the sopapillas are still hot, sprinkle both sides with a generous coating of cinnamon-sugar. Serve hot.

HOLIDAY BRUNCH

In the excitement of the holidays, evening meals get a lot more attention than morning meals. This year, why not try a reversal? Make the day a long, festive occasion starting with a pull-out-all-the-stops brunch for family and friends. Serves 8.

Snowmen Breads
Honey-Baked Apples
Molasses and Mustard-
** Glazed Breakfast Ham**
Creamy Confetti Eggs

Freshly squeezed pink
* grapefruit juice*
Butter, honey, jams, and
* preserves*
Fancy cookies

SNOWMEN BREADS

Traditional at Christmas in Switzerland and Germany, these big, puffy breads are delicious and fun to make. Tie a bright ribbon around each one and serve them with sweet butter, honey, and assorted jams and marmalades.

1	pkg. active dry yeast (2 1/2 tsp. (12 mL))	1
3/4 cup	lukewarm milk	175 mL
1/3 cup + 1 tsp.	sugar	80 mL
3 1/2-4 1/2 cups	all-purpose flour	875 mL-1.25 L
2 tsp.	finely grated orange rind	10 mL
1 tsp.	salt	5 mL
1 tbsp.	ground nutmeg	15 mL
4	eggs, at room temperature	4
1/3 cup	softened butter	75 mL
40	dried currants	40
2 tbsp.	milk	30 mL

In a warm bowl, sprinkle the yeast over the milk to soften. Stir in 1 tsp. (5 mL) of the sugar, stir, and cover. Let stand 5 minutes until the yeast bubbles and foams. Stir smooth.

In an electric mixer, combine the yeast mixture with 1 3/4 cups (425 mL) of the flour, the remaining 1/3 cup (75 mL) sugar, the orange rind, salt, nutmeg, 3 of the eggs, and the butter. Beat 2 minutes. (The mixture will be batter-like.) Add 1 3/4 cups (425 mL) of the remaining flour, and more flour as necessary, a little at a time, until the dough is soft and springy and just cleans the sides of the bowl. Cover with plastic wrap and a clean cloth, and set in a warm spot to double in size, about 45 minutes.

Stir the dough down, knead on a lightly floured surface 2 minutes, and divide into 8 equal pieces. Lightly grease several baking sheets (or line with baking parchment). For each snowman, use half the piece of dough to make a 4 inch (10 cm) long oval for the body. With a little more than half the remaining dough, make a round, flattened ball for the head. Pinch off a tiny round for the nose. Divide the remaining dough into 2 arms and 2 legs, each 1 inch (2.5 cm) long. With a bit of water, join the parts of the snowman. Press 2 currants into the head for eyes and 3 currants down the front for buttons.

Place the snowmen 3 inches (7.5 cm) apart on the baking sheets. Let rise in a warm spot 30-40 minutes, until almost doubled. Heat the oven to 350°F (180°C). Beat the remaining egg with the 2 tbsp. (30 mL) milk and brush this glaze over each snowman. Bake 15 minutes or until puffed and golden brown. Cool on wire racks 30 minutes before serving.

The Easy Gourmet features a photograph of this recipe on page 17.

HONEY-BAKED APPLES

Serve these comforting breakfast treats warm in pretty bowls. They are lovely all by themselves, and even better topped with whipped cream.

8	large Rome beauty apples	8
1/3 cup	*each* prepared granola, raisins or currants, and diced walnuts or almonds	75 mL
1/2 tsp.	*each* ground cinnamon and nutmeg	2 mL
	grated rind of 1 lemon	
2 tbsp.	lemon juice	30 mL
1/2 cup	honey	125 mL
1 cup	apple juice	250 mL
4 tbsp.	butter	60 mL
	whipping cream, chilled or softly whipped	

Wash and core the apples. With a vegetable peeler, peel one continuous strip from the circumference of each. Slice a thin piece off the bottom so they will stand level in a baking dish. Heat the oven to 350°F (180°C).

Place the apples upright in a rectangular glass baking dish with the sides almost touching. Combine the granola, raisins, nuts, cinnamon, nutmeg, and lemon rind. Toss to combine thoroughly and divide the filling among the centres of the 8 apples. Pack the filling down lightly. Combine the lemon juice, honey, apple juice, and butter in a small saucepan and bring the mixture to a bubbly simmer, about 5 minutes. Pour over the apples. Cover with foil and bake 30 minutes.

Uncover the apples and bake until very tender, about 30 minutes longer, basting frequently with the syrup. Cool to warm or room temperature, place in individual serving bowls, and top with cream.

The Easy Gourmet features a photograph of this recipe on page 17.

MOLASSES AND MUSTARD-GLAZED BREAKFAST HAM

Festive appearance, wonderful aromas, good eating, almost no fuss—what more could you want in a holiday brunch entrée?

1	butt end half of smoked ham, fully cooked	1
	(6-8 lbs. (3-4 kg))	
	whole cloves for decoration	
1 cup	brown sugar, packed	250 mL
1/3 cup	*each* molasses and Dijon-style mustard	75 mL
1/2 tsp.	*each* ground allspice and cinnamon	2 mL
2 tbsp.	cider vinegar	30 mL
1/2 cup	fine bread crumbs	125 mL
1/2 cup	water or apple juice	125 mL

With a small, sharp knife, remove the heavy rind from the ham, leaving about 1/2 inch (1 cm) of white fat. Score the fat in diagonal lines 1/2 inch (1 cm) apart, in two directions, to make a diamond pattern. Insert 1 whole clove in the centre of each diamond. Heat the oven to 325°F (160°C).

In a small cup, combine the brown sugar, molasses, mustard, allspice, cinnamon, and vinegar. Brush this glaze evenly over the ham. Sprinkle evenly with the bread crumbs. Place the ham in an open roaster lined with foil or baking parchment. Carefully pour the water around the ham in the bottom of the roaster. Roast for 1-1 1/2 hours, or until heated through and rich golden brown. Remove from the oven and allow to rest 20 minutes for the juices to re-absorb. Carve on a warmed platter, leaving a bit of the crunchy glazed crust on each slice.

The Easy Gourmet features a photograph of this recipe on page 17.

CREAMY CONFETTI EGGS

Made for entertaining, these eggs stay soft on a warming dish for up to 30 minutes. The red and green peppers are the perfect holiday touch.

10 tbsp.	butter	150 mL
2	*each* large red and green bell peppers, diced	2
1 tsp.	sugar	5 mL
	salt and pepper to taste	
2 tbsp.	all-purpose flour	30 mL
1 cup	sour cream	250 mL
24	eggs, at room temperature	24
1 tsp.	salt	5 mL
1/4 tsp.	cracked black pepper	1 mL
1/4 cup	minced fresh parsley	50 mL

Melt 2 tbsp. (30 mL) of the butter in a large, non-stick skillet over medium-high heat. Add the peppers and sauté, stirring, until softened. Sprinkle with the sugar and sauté until pale golden. Season with salt and pepper to taste. Set aside. Heat 4 tbsp. (60 mL) of the remaining butter in a small saucepan until bubbly. Add the flour and cook 2 minutes, whisking constantly, until bubbly and cooked. Remove from the heat, stir in the sour cream, and whisk smooth. Return to very low heat and warm through 1 minute. Set aside.

Beat the eggs with the 1 tsp. (5 mL) salt and 1/4 tsp. (1 mL) pepper. Heat the remaining 4 tbsp. (60 mL) butter in a wide, non-stick skillet over medium heat. When the butter is sizzling and foamy, pour in the eggs. As the eggs cook, push the cooked portion to the centre of the pan, allowing the uncooked portion to flow underneath. When almost set but not dry, sprinkle with minced parsley. Remove from the heat and stir in the sour cream mixture. Mound the eggs on a heated platter and top with the sautéed peppers. Serve at once, or keep warm up to 30 minutes on a warming tray.

The Easy Gourmet features a photograph of this recipe on page 17.

Opposite: (counter-clockwise from top left) Holiday Brunch (pp. 13-16)— Snowmen Breads, Honey Baked Apples, Molasses and Mustard-Glazed Breakfast Ham, Creamy Confetti Eggs.

HARVEST FARM BRUNCH

Here is a hearty, down-home brunch, all served around a wooden kitchen table dressed in simple linens, a gingham cloth, or rustic placemats. Bring everything to the table at once and invite your guests to "dig in." Now this is the way to start a big day! Serves 6.

Country Apple Pancake
Granola Breakfast Bread
Sugar-Peppered Brunch
  Bacon

Freshly squeezed orange juice
Creamy scrambled eggs
Crisp breakfast link sausages

COUNTRY APPLE PANCAKE

This enormous oven-baked country pancake is a delight. Serve right from the skillet in big wedges, with a dusting of powdered sugar and your favourite pancake syrup. Grilled sausages are the perfect accompaniment.

6 tbsp.	butter	90 mL
2	large apples, peeled, cored, and sliced into thin wedges (Granny Smith, Golden Delicious, or McIntosh)	2
3 tbsp.	sugar	45 mL
1/2 tsp.	ground cinnamon	2 mL
1 tbsp.	lemon juice	15 mL
4	eggs, at room temperature	4
2/3 cup	*each* all-purpose flour and milk	150 mL
	grated rind of 1 lemon	
2 tbsp.	melted butter	30 mL
	icing sugar for dusting	

Melt 3 tbsp. (45 mL) of the butter in a large skillet over medium-high heat. Add the apple slices and sauté, tossing, 2-3 minutes. Sprinkle on the sugar, cinnamon, and lemon juice. Turn the heat to high and sauté 2-3 minutes more. The apples should be pale golden, yet still tender, and hold their shape. Set the apples aside up to 1 hour.

Heat the oven to 425°F (220°C). Prepare the batter by whisking together the eggs, flour, milk, lemon rind, and melted butter (or use a blender or food processor). Beat until the batter is very smooth. In a large, non-stick, ovenproof skillet, heat the remaining 3 tbsp. (45 mL) butter until melted and bubbly. Spread the prepared apples evenly over the bottom of the skillet. Pour the batter over the apples. Bake in the centre of the oven 20-25 minutes, or until golden brown and puffy.

Remove the pancake from the oven. Dust the top with sifted icing sugar and serve at once, cut in thick wedges, accompanied by your choice of syrup.

The Easy Gourmet features a photograph of this recipe on page 35.

GRANOLA BREAKFAST BREAD

This is a hearty, chewy, healthy breakfast bread—simple to make from pantry-shelf ingredients. Any kind of granola can be used, so go ahead and experiment. Serve fresh from the oven or toasted the next day, accompanied by sweet butter and marmalade.

1/2 cup	lukewarm water	125 mL
1 tbsp.	brown sugar	15 mL
2	pkgs. active dry yeast (5 tsp. (25 mL))	2
2 cups	milk, scalded and cooled to room temperature	500 mL
2 tbsp.	softened butter or safflower oil	30 mL
1 tbsp.	*each* finely grated orange and lemon rind	15 mL
1 1/2 tsp.	salt	7 mL
1/2 cup	*each* oat bran and brown sugar	125 mL
1/2 cup + 4 tbsp.	quick-cooking oats	185 mL
2 cups	granola (your favourite kind)	500 mL
2 cups	whole wheat flour	500 mL
2 3/4 - 3 cups	all-purpose flour	675-750 mL

Place the water in a large mixing bowl and stir in the brown sugar. Sprinkle on the yeast, cover, and let stand 5 minutes to soften. (The yeast will "bubble and foam" if it is active.) Stir the mixture down. Stir in the milk, butter, citrus rind, salt, oat bran, brown sugar, 1/2 cup (125 mL) of the oats, and the granola. Allow to soak 5 minutes.

Beat in the whole wheat flour until smooth. Begin adding the all-purpose flour, 1 cup (250 mL) at a time, adding only enough flour to produce a soft dough that just cleans the sides of the bowl. Knead the dough on a floured surface 5 minutes until elastic and springy. Place the dough in a buttered or oiled bowl, turn to coat, and cover with plastic wrap and a clean towel. Let rise in a warm place until doubled in bulk, about 1 hour.

Punch the dough down, turn out and divide in half. Knead each piece 1-2 minutes, then tuck the ends under neatly. Place each half in a greased loaf pan 9 x 5 x 3 inches (23 x 13 x 7.5 cm). Brush the tops of the loaves lightly with water or milk and sprinkle each with 2 tbsp. (30 mL) oats. Let rise to the tops of the pans. Heat the oven to 350°F (180°C).

Bake in the lower third of the oven 45 minutes, or until rich golden brown. Cool on a wire rack at least 1 hour before slicing with a sharp, thin-bladed, serrated knife.

The Easy Gourmet features a photograph of this recipe on page 35.

SUGAR-PEPPERED BRUNCH BACON

Here is a great way to prepare morning bacon for a crowd. The secret? A sprinkling of brown sugar and coarse cracked black pepper—delicious!

1 lb.	sliced bacon (thick-sliced or regular)	500 g
	brown sugar to taste	
	cracked black pepper to taste	

Place the bacon on a rack over a pan. Heat the oven to 400°F (200°C). Lightly sprinkle the bacon with brown sugar and cracked black pepper to taste. Bake the bacon 10-20 minutes, without turning, until crispy and golden brown. Serve piping hot.

The Easy Gourmet features a photograph of this recipe on page 35.

C OUNTRY FRENCH OMELETTE PARTY

This perfectly light and satisfying brunch is the occasion to bring out your prettiest crockery plates and mugs, colourful floral linens, and a pitcher of bright fresh-cut flowers. Add good conversation and a selection of weekend newspapers, and voilà—a comfortable and memorable shared meal. Serves 6-10.

Baked Brie en Croute
Omelettes aux Fines Herbes

Assorted preserves, conserves, chutney, and applesauce
Leafy green salad
Hot baguettes with sweet butter
Café au lait

BAKED BRIE EN CROUTE

This is a stunning yet oh-so-simple appetizer: a whole brie cheese, baked in golden brown puff pastry. Serve warm, and accompany with your favourite chutney, assorted fruit preserves, or chilled applesauce.

1	14 oz. (400 g) pkg. frozen puff pastry, thawed	1
1	whole round brie cheese, 8 inches (20 cm) in diameter, about 2 lbs. (1 kg)	1
1	egg, beaten	1

Cut off one-third of the thawed pastry and set aside. On a lightly floured surface, roll out the larger piece of pastry into a 10 1/2 inch (26 cm) circle. Place the whole brie in the centre of the circle. Roll out the reserved pastry into an 8 inch (20 cm) circle and place on top of the brie. Bring up the edges of the bottom pastry round to enclose the sides of the cheese. Join the edges of the two pastry rounds all around the top of the cheese, by pinching the dough together with your fingers. Crimp, if desired, into a pretty V-shaped pattern all around. Transfer the pastry-wrapped cheese carefully onto a baking sheet lined with a sheet of baking parchment. Chill 1 hour, or up to 24 hours, uncovered.

Heat the oven to 375°F (190°C). Lightly brush the pastry top and sides with the beaten egg. Take care not to allow any egg to run underneath the pastry. Bake on the centre rack of the heated oven about 30-35 minutes, or until the pastry is a rich golden brown. (If the pastry puffs too much during baking, prick several places very lightly, through the crust only, to deflate slightly.) Cool to room temperature, about 30 minutes. With a sharp, serrated knife, cut into wedges and serve.

OMELETTES AUX FINES HERBES

Fresh herbed omelettes are a delight, and today's produce section offers an abundant selection of fresh herbs all year round. The secret to great omelettes is to prepare each one quickly in a sizzling hot skillet.

4 tbsp.	*each* minced fresh chives and thinly sliced green onion	60 mL
2	cloves garlic, pressed	2
2 tbsp.	*each* minced fresh tarragon, thyme, basil, and parsley	30 mL
12	eggs, at room temperature	12
3 tbsp.	ice-cold water	45 mL
1 tsp.	salt	5 mL
	freshly ground black pepper to taste	
9 tbsp.	butter	135 mL

Toss together the chives, green onions, garlic, and herbs. In a large bowl, whisk together the eggs, water, and salt. Season with pepper.

To cook *each* omelette, heat the skillet over medium-high heat until hot. Add 1 1/2 tbsp. (22 mL) of the butter to the skillet, and when it is melted and foamy, ladle in one-sixth of the egg mixture. Allow the eggs to set 5 seconds. Push the cooked portion in towards the centre of the skillet, allowing the uncooked egg to flow underneath. Sprinkle 2 tbsp. (30 mL) of the herb mixture over the omelette. Cook the omelette about 1 minute longer until the bottom is set and the top is moist and creamy. The total cooking time should not exceed 2 minutes.

Holding the skillet at a 45° angle, allow half the omelette to slide onto a warmed serving plate. Turn the skillet over and tip so that the other half folds over. Serve at once. Repeat the procedure for each omelette.

Note: If you substitute dried herbs for fresh, use one-third the amount shown in these directions.

SUNRISE SPECIAL

Here is a menu for a special-occasion brunch or breakfast: fresh, bright, and pretty, and so versatile it is equally at home on a linen-dressed table or on a breakfast tray. The big bonus is it's easy enough for beginning cooks. So treat someone you love to a simple, elegant, good-morning meal. Serves 4.

Orange Blossom   Fresh bakery cookies and
Shrimp and Scallop Frittata   *croissants*
Fruit Ambrosia

ORANGE BLOSSOM

Creamy, rich, and smooth, this is a drink that will be in demand for seconds, so make plenty.

2 cups	cold orange juice	500 mL
1 cup	cold half-and-half cream	250 mL
4 scoops	vanilla or orange ice cream	4 scoops

Pour the orange juice and cream into a blender and mix briefly. Add the ice cream and blend until thick and creamy. Pour into glasses and serve immediately.

SHRIMP AND SCALLOP FRITTATA

This simple, quick dish is perfectly delicious and loaded with protein.

2 tbsp.	olive oil	30 mL
2 tbsp.	butter	30 mL
1/2 lb.	medium raw shrimp, peeled	250 g
1/2 lb.	large raw scallops, halved	250 g
3-4	green onions, sliced or chopped	3-4
6	eggs, well beaten	6
	salt and pepper to taste	

Heat the broiler.

Heat the oil and butter in an 8 inch (20 cm) heavy ovenproof skillet. If you do not have an ovenproof skillet, a regular pan handle can be protected with several layers of aluminum foil. Add the shrimp and cook until just barely pink. Add the scallops and cook a few minutes longer, just until opaque. Add the onions and cook 1 minute longer.

Pour the beaten eggs over everything and cook until the egg mixture begins to look done around the edges. The mixture can be lifted gently from time to time at the edges to allow some of the uncooked egg to flow underneath.

When the frittata is almost firm, finish the dish by placing it under the broiler until the top turns golden brown and the eggs puff at the edges. This will take about 10 minutes from start to finish.

Slip the frittata onto a serving plate. Sprinkle on a little salt and pepper and cut into wedges to serve.

FRUIT AMBROSIA

Any of your favourite seasonal fruits can be substituted for the ones suggested here. Whatever you put in, a sweet, light, fresh dessert is the result.

1/2	honeydew melon or cantaloupe	1/2
1	mandarin orange	1
1	nectarine	1
1	red apple	1
1 cup	water	250 mL
1/2 cup	sugar	125 mL
	grapes or berries for garnish	

Peel the melon, orange, and nectarine. Cut into cubes or wedges and place in a medium bowl. Core and cut up the apple, leaving the skin on.

In a medium saucepan, bring the water and sugar to a boil over medium heat. Reduce the heat and let simmer 5 minutes. Chill.

Pour the chilled sweet syrup over the fruit and refrigerate until ready to serve. (The dish may be made ahead to this point and stored 3-4 days.)

At serving time, spoon into serving dishes and garnish with grapes or berries.

# **L**OVERS' BRUNCH

This is the menu for a perfect sweetheart of a brunch. The occasion? Your private celebration. The guests? Just you and your sweetheart. A gorgeous ensemble of tempting colours, tastes, and textures, this at-home brunch is the cook's way of saying "I love you." Serves 2.

Mock Champagne Cocktail   Steamed baby asparagus spears
Cheesy Popovers with
  Creamy Eggs
Chocolate-Raspberry Cup

MOCK CHAMPAGNE COCKTAIL

Cool and refreshing, this is a tasty alcohol-free drink for any occasion.

	ice cubes	
2 cups	cold, freshly squeezed orange juice	500 mL
1 cup	chilled club soda	250 mL
	sprigs of fresh mint for garnish	

Fill 2 tall champagne flutes with ice cubes. Divide the orange juice between the glasses and top up with the soda. Garnish with mint and serve.

CHEESY POPOVERS WITH CREAMY EGGS

Popovers are a classic and a favourite, and they are wonderfully versatile. This version has creamy scrambled eggs spooned inside and over the top. For an extra dash, garnish with cooked fresh asparagus.

5	eggs	5
3/4 cup	milk	175 mL
pinch	salt	pinch
3/4 cup	all-purpose flour	175 mL
3 tbsp.	shredded cheddar cheese	45 mL
1 tbsp.	butter	15 mL
2 tbsp.	chopped onion	30 mL
2 tbsp.	chopped tomato or red bell pepper	30 mL

Grease 4 custard cups, 6 oz. (180 mL) each. Beat 2 of the eggs with the milk and salt. Add the flour and beat until smooth. Make sure the mixture is at room temperature. Stir in the cheese. Spoon into the custard cups. Bake at 425°F (220°C) for 30 minutes or until well puffed and dark brown.

About 5 minutes before the popovers are done, melt the butter in a medium skillet and sauté the onion until tender. Add the tomato and cook another 1-2 minutes. Pour in the eggs and gently stir and lift until the eggs are firm but still soft.

Remove the popovers from the custard cups and place on a serving plate. Break open the top of each and spoon over the soft cooked scrambled eggs.

CHOCOLATE-RASPBERRY CUP

"Sweets for the sweet"—the expression was made for desserts like this! Prepared meringue cups from the bakery save a step and add a touch of elegance.

2	medium meringue cups	2
2 scoops	deluxe vanilla ice cream	2 scoops
4 tbsp.	sugar	60 mL
4 tbsp.	light corn syrup	60 mL
2 tbsp.	cocoa	30 mL
2 tbsp.	half-and-half cream	30 mL
1/2 tsp.	vanilla	2 mL
pinch	salt	pinch
dash	Angustora bitters (optional)	dash
1/2 cup	fresh raspberries	125 mL

Place a meringue cup on each serving plate. Spoon in the ice cream. Keep in the refrigerator until serving time.

In a medium saucepan, mix together the sugar, corn syrup, cocoa, cream, vanilla, salt, and bitters. Bring to a boil over medium heat and cook for 3 minutes. Remove from the heat. (The dish may be made ahead to this point and allowed to cool. It will thicken as it stands. To reheat, warm gently [do not boil]).

When ready to serve, divide the raspberries between the dessert plates and spoon on the warm chocolate sauce. Serve immediately.

SUNDAY BRUNCH

In keeping with the spirit of the holiday season, when everyone is relaxed and happy, make life easy for yourself—let your home fill with the spicy scent of Mulled Apple Punch while you put the finishing touches on the dishes you've prepared ahead. Guaranteed to get any special day off to a great start! Serves 8.

Mulled Apple Punch
Hot Seafood Salad
Puffy Chili Rellenos
Silver Dollar Pancakes
Dreamy, Creamy Cheesecake

Whole smoked salmon and crackers from the deli

MULLED APPLE PUNCH

When this spicy, fruity punch is simmering on the stove, your house will fill up with the wonderful aromas of holiday time. Make this punch once and it will become a tradition. Makes 24 cups (6 L).

2 qts.	apple juice	2 L
2 qts.	cranberry cocktail	2 L
2 qts.	orange juice	2 L
1	whole cinnamon stick	1
6	whole cloves	6
	slices of orange or lemon for garnish	

Put all the ingredients in a large saucepan and bring to a slow simmer. Serve hot with a slice of orange or lemon.

HOT SEAFOOD SALAD

Warm seafood salad is a light, healthy, and scrumptious addition to the holiday table. Serve it on bright green lettuce leaves for an extra festive touch.

1 tbsp.	butter	15 mL
2 cups	sliced celery	500 mL
1/2 cup	chopped onion	125 mL
1/2 lb.	fresh mushrooms, sliced	250 g
1	red bell pepper, chopped	1
1	8 oz. (227 mL) can water chestnuts, drained and sliced	1
1/2 lb.	fresh cooked crab meat	250 g
1/2 lb.	fresh cooked shrimp	250 g
1 cup	mayonnaise	250 mL
6	hard-cooked eggs, sliced	6
1 tsp.	paprika	5 mL
1 tsp.	freshly ground pepper	5 mL
1/2 cup	buttered bread crumbs	125 mL
	lettuce leaves for garnish	

Melt the butter in a medium skillet and sauté the celery, onions, mushrooms, and pepper until tender, about 5 minutes.

In a medium bowl, mix together the water chestnuts, crab, shrimp, mayonnaise, eggs, paprika, and pepper. Stir in the cooked vegetables.

Place in a greased 3 quart (3 L) casserole and top with the bread crumbs. Bake at 350°F (180°C) for 30 minutes or until the dish is heated through and the topping is browned. Serve on lettuce leaves.

PUFFY CHILI RELLENOS

Chiles add their unbeatable south-of-the-border tang to this puffy, light, quiche-like dish.

1	9 inch (23 cm) unbaked pie crust	1
2 cups	shredded Monterey jack cheese	500 mL
2	4 oz. (114 g) cans whole green chiles, drained and sliced	2
6	eggs	6
1/2 cup	half-and-half cream	125 mL
dash	bottled hot pepper sauce	dash
pinch	nutmeg	pinch

Heat the oven to 425°F (220°C). Cover the pie crust with a layer of foil and press into the shell. Hold the foil down with a layer of dried beans or peas. Bake 5-7 minutes. Remove the foil and beans. (This is called baking blind.)

Cover the partially baked crust with 1 cup (250 mL) of the cheese. Spread on half the chiles. Repeat with the remaining cheese and chiles.

In a medium bowl, beat together 4 of the eggs, the cream, hot pepper sauce, and nutmeg. Pour over the chiles and cheese and bake at 375°F (190°C) for 30 minutes.

Separate the remaining 2 eggs. In a small bowl, beat the 2 egg whites until soft peaks form. Lightly beat the 2 yolks and gently fold them into the whites. Spread over the hot chiles and cheese and bake 15 minutes longer or until the top is puffy and browned.

SILVER DOLLAR PANCAKES

A tiny, savoury pancake, this delicacy is served topped with bright red or black caviar.

2 cups	all-purpose flour	500 mL
1/3 cup	sugar	75 mL
4 tsp.	baking powder	20 mL
1 tsp.	salt	5 mL
2 cups	milk	500 mL
2	eggs, separated	2
1	green onion, finely chopped	1
1 tbsp.	butter or oil	15 mL
	caviar and sour cream for topping	

In a medium bowl, stir together the flour, sugar, baking powder, and salt. In another bowl, mix together the milk and egg yolks. In a small bowl, beat the egg whites until soft peaks form.

Quickly and gently stir the milk mixture into the flour mixture. Fold in the egg whites and stir in the green onion.

Heat the butter in a medium non-stick skillet and, using a small 2 tbsp. (30 mL) scoop, spoon the batter into the pan. Each pancake should be about the size of a silver dollar. Fry until golden on each side. Cool on wire racks.

Serve with bowls of caviar and sour cream.

DREAMY, CREAMY CHEESECAKE

Be sure to make this dish at least a day before serving so it can chill thoroughly and the flavours can blend. Then get ready to share the recipe with your guests!

2 cups	graham cracker crumbs	500 mL
1/2 cup + 2 tbsp.	butter	155 mL
1	8 oz. (250 g) pkg. cream cheese	1
3	eggs, separated	3
3/4 cup	sugar	175 mL
1 cup	sour cream	250 mL
1 tbsp.	vanilla	15 mL
1/2 cup	whipping cream	125 mL
3 tbsp.	icing sugar	45 mL
	red and green maraschino cherries for garnish	

Line an 8 inch (20 cm) springform pan, or other pan with 2 inch (5 cm) straight sides, with foil. Leave the foil edges overlapping so that you can use them to lift the cake out of the pan. Grease well.

Mix the crumbs with 1/2 cup (125 mL) of the butter and press lightly into the bottom and sides of the pan.

Beat together the cream cheese and the remaining 2 tbsp. (30 mL) butter. Add the egg yolks and sugar. Stir in the sour cream and vanilla. Beat the whites until soft peaks form and gently fold into the mixture. Pour over the crumbs in the pan. Bake at 325°F (160°C) for exactly 35 minutes. Let cool in the oven, with the door closed, about 1 hour (this will help set the cake). Don't worry about any cracks on the surface—the whipped cream topping will cover them up. Chill in the refrigerator before releasing from the pan.

Just before serving, whip the cream with the icing sugar and carefully spread over the top. Scatter on chopped red and green maraschino cherries and serve.

WEDDING BRUNCH

Pink and white are the theme colours for this wedding brunch, an event for close family and friends who gather before or after the wedding to honour the bride and groom. These are busy days, so the recipes are designed for make-ahead convenience. Serves 16.

Wedding Punch
Individual Mini Shrimp
  Quiches
24-Hour Vegetable Salad
Spectacular Ham and Egg Bake
Wedding Party Cake

Hot butterflake rolls with fresh butter

WEDDING PUNCH

This is a rich, ruby-coloured punch, garnished with an ice ring of fresh fruit. Beautiful on the table and delicious to sip, it is the ideal refreshment for any reception. Makes 54 servings, 1/2 cup (125 mL) each.

2	red apples	2
2	green apples	2
	juice of 1 lemon	
3	small clusters grapes	3
10 cups	clear apple juice	2.5 L
1 cup	water	250 mL
2 qts.	grape juice	2 L
3 qts.	club soda	3 L
	sprigs of fresh mint for garnish	

To prepare the ice ring, slice the red and green apples and toss with the lemon juice to prevent browning. Arrange with grape clusters in an attractive design in a ring mold. Mix 2 cups (500 mL) of the apple juice with the water and pour into the mold until the liquid half covers the fruit. Freeze. Add the remaining apple juice-water mixture and freeze until serving time.

In a large punch bowl, mix the remaining 8 cups (2 L) of the apple juice with the grape juice. Top up with club soda. Unmold the ice ring and float it fruit side up in the punch. Garnish with fresh mint.

INDIVIDUAL MINI SHRIMP QUICHES

This delectable dish is a real time-saver as well. Just bake the tart shells and mix up the filling the day before, and bake the quiches just before serving.

36	frozen mini tarts	36
1/2 lb.	fresh cooked shrimp	250 g
4	eggs	4
1 cup	small-curd cottage cheese	250 mL
4 tbsp.	grated Parmesan cheese	60 mL
4 tbsp.	chopped chives or green onion	60 mL
dash	bottled hot pepper sauce	dash
pinch	freshly ground black pepper	pinch
1 cup	shredded Monterey jack cheese	250 mL

Heat the oven to 375°F (190°C). Bake the tarts on a baking sheet for 5 minutes. Push down any dough that may have puffed in the centre. Set aside.

Saving 36 perfect shrimp for garnish, coarsely chop the remainder. Beat together the eggs and cottage cheese. Stir in the chopped shrimp, Parmesan cheese, chives, hot pepper sauce, and pepper.

When ready to bake, heat the oven to 375°F (190°C). Spoon the shrimp mixture into the tart shells. Top with shredded cheese and reserved shrimp. (Any leftover mixture can be refrigerated up to 1 day.) Bake 20-25 minutes or until puffed and golden.

Opposite: Harvest Farm Brunch (pp. 19-21)—(top right to bottom) Granola Breakfast Bread, Country Apple Pancake, Sugar-Peppered Brunch Bacon.

24-HOUR VEGETABLE SALAD

Layers of fresh, colourful vegetables in a big glass bowl make this salad as gorgeous as it is delicious. Dig deep when serving to get a little of everything.

1	head iceberg lettuce	1
3	Belgian endive	3
2	carrots, peeled	2
1	large red bell pepper	1
6	green onions	6
1	bunch radishes	1
1 cup	frozen, tiny green peas	250 mL
1 cup	mayonnaise	250 mL
3/4 cup	chili sauce	175 mL

Thinly shred the lettuce, endive, and carrots. Thinly slice the pepper, green onions, and radishes. Place half the lettuce on the bottom of a large glass salad bowl. Layer the remaining ingredients alternately with the peas. Top with the remaining half of the lettuce. Mix together the mayonnaise and chili sauce and spread over top to seal the lettuce underneath. Cover and chill 24 hours.

SPECTACULAR HAM AND EGG BAKE

Here is a colourful, puffy baked dish made with the natural go-togethers of ham, cheese, eggs, and bell peppers. The Red Pepper Sauce gives the dish a gorgeous, distinctively-flavoured finish.

2	medium red bell peppers	2
1 lb.	shredded Black Forest ham	500 g
1 tbsp.	Dijon mustard	15 mL
1 tbsp.	butter	15 mL
2	10 oz. (300 g) pkgs. frozen chopped spinach, thawed and squeezed dry	2
3 tbsp.	chopped onion	45 mL
1 tsp.	freshly grated nutmeg	5 mL
6-8	slices firm white bread, crusts removed	6-8
1/2 lb.	sliced Swiss cheese	250 mL
6	eggs	6
2 cups	milk	500 mL
	Red Pepper Sauce (recipe follows)	

Thinly slice the peppers and set aside. Mix the shredded ham with the mustard and set aside. Melt the butter in a medium skillet and sauté the spinach and onion until tender, about 3-4 minutes. Season with nutmeg. Set aside.

Trim the bread to fit the bottom of a 10 inch (25 cm) springform pan. If your pan does not have a removable bottom, or it does not have a close seal, line with foil, overlapping the edges so that it can be removed easily.

Line the bottom of the pan with half the bread. Layer on half the peppers, ham, spinach, and cheese. Repeat with the remaining bread, peppers, ham, spinach, and cheese.

Mix together the eggs and milk and pour over all. Let stand 10 minutes before baking.

Heat the oven to 400°F (200°C). Bake 50 minutes or until a knife inserted slightly off centre comes out clean and the cheese is melted and bubbling. Let rest 10 minutes before removing the sides of the pan. Place on a large serving platter and slice into wedges. Serve with Red Pepper Sauce.

If you are preparing the dish ahead, take it from the refrigerator and bake 20 minutes or until heated through.

RED PEPPER SAUCE

Wonderfully red and smoky-tasting, this sauce gets its special taste from red peppers grilled under the broiler. Makes 3 cups (750 mL).

2 lbs.	red bell peppers	1 kg
3 tbsp.	olive oil	45 mL
1	medium onion, sliced	1
1	clove garlic, minced	1
1/2 tsp.	salt	2 mL
pinch	cayenne	pinch
1/2-1 tsp.	fresh thyme	2-5 mL
	juice of 1/2 lemon	
	whipping cream (optional)	

Place the peppers on a foil-lined baking sheet and broil, turning, until blackened on all sides. Remove from the broiler, place in a brown paper bag, and let steam for 10 minutes. Under cold running water, peel off the skin and strip away the seeds.

Heat the oil and sauté the onion until tender. Add the garlic and cook for 1 minute. Add the peppers and the remaining ingredients and simmer, covered, until the peppers are very soft, about 45-50 minutes.

Cool slightly. Purée in a food processor or blender until smooth. If necessary, press through a sieve or food mill to remove any bits of skin that may remain. Taste and adjust seasonings.

The sauce may be refrigerated for up to 2 weeks or frozen for 6 months. If too thick, thin out with a little cream. Serve hot.

WEDDING PARTY CAKE

This is a lovely, light, festive cake. Served without the optional whipped cream topping, it is also a calorie-watchers' delight.

1	baked 10 inch (25 cm) angel food cake	1
2	3 oz. (85 g) pkgs. raspberry jelly powder	2
1/2 cup	boiling water	125 mL
1	12 1/2 oz. (355 mL) can frozen raspberry concentrate	1
6	egg whites	6
1/2 cup	sugar	125 mL
1 cup	whipping cream (optional)	250 mL
2 tbsp.	icing sugar (optional)	30 mL
drop	red food colouring (optional)	drop

Trim the crusts from the angel food cake and tear into bite-sized pieces. Place in a large bowl and set aside.

In a medium saucepan, sprinkle the jelly powder into the boiling water. Place over low heat until the powder is dissolved, about 2 minutes.

Pour into a bowl, stir in the raspberry concentrate, and cool until the mixture mounds slightly when dropped from a spoon, about 45 minutes at room temperature or 20 minutes in the refrigerator. Watch the mixture carefully if cooling in the refrigerator as it will set quickly once it starts to gel.

Beat the egg whites until soft peaks form. Gradually add the sugar, beating until stiff and glossy. Fold into the raspberry mixture. Spoon one-quarter of this mixture into the bottom of a large, lightly oiled angel food or bundt pan. Pour the remainder over the reserved angel food cake pieces and stir to coat. Pour into the mold and press down lightly. Chill overnight. (The dish may be frozen at this point.)

When ready to serve, invert onto a large platter. Whip the cream with the icing sugar until soft peaks form. Add the food colouring, allowing the colouring to streak the cream. Spread over the top and sides of the cake.

RIENDS' BRUNCH

Cooking for friends is a great way to express your appreciation, and this menu lets you serve a delicious, attractive brunch and still have lots of time for those special people. Prepare the dishes in advance, choose pale pinks and greens for the linens and flowers, do your last-minute heat-ups in the microwave, and relax! Serves 8-10.

Hot Tomato Clam Slipper
Sour Cream Shrimp Curry
Green Rice
Mushrooms Oregano

Green salad with lemon
dressing
Assorted muffins

HOT TOMATO CLAM SLIPPER

Warm and spicy, this drink is a delicious start to a special brunch. It's also "spike-able"—add a dash of vodka just before serving.

8 cups	clamato juice	2 L
1/2 tsp.	salt	2 mL
1/2 tsp.	celery salt	2 mL
1/2 tsp.	ground thyme	2 mL
1/2 tsp.	black pepper	2 mL
1/4 tsp.	garlic powder	1 mL
	celery salt to taste	
8-10	celery sticks	8-10

Combine the clamato juice, salt, 1/2 tsp. (2 mL) celery salt, thyme, pepper, and garlic powder in a microproof jug or dish.

Microwave on MEDIUM 50% power 20-25 minutes until hot, stirring once or twice during the cooking time. If you are using a probe, program to 160°F at MEDIUM 50% power level.

To serve, moisten the rim of each glass and dip in celery salt. Pop a celery stick into each and serve warm.

SOUR CREAM SHRIMP CURRY

Served with Green Rice (recipe follows) this dish makes a colourful and soul-satisfying addition to the brunch table. To save time, you can assemble it in advance and reheat just before serving.

1/2 cup	slivered almonds	125 mL
6 tbsp.	butter	90 mL
1 cup	finely chopped green onion	250 mL
1/2 cup	finely chopped green bell pepper	125 mL
1	clove garlic, crushed	1
2 cups	thinly sliced mushrooms	500 mL
3 tsp.	curry powder	15 mL
1 tsp.	salt	5 mL
1/4 tsp.	white pepper	1 mL
1 tsp.	Worcestershire sauce	5 mL
1/2 tsp.	dry mustard	2 mL
2 cups	sour cream	500 mL
1 lb.	cooked shrimp	500 g

Place the almonds and 2 tbsp. (30 mL) of the butter in a microproof dish. Microwave on HIGH 100% power in 1 minute increments until the almonds are a golden brown, stirring after each cooking period. Set aside.

Place the remaining 4 tbsp. (60 mL) butter, green onion, green pepper, and garlic in a large microproof casserole dish. Cover and microwave on HIGH 100% power 2 minutes. Stir in the mushrooms, curry powder, salt, white pepper, Worcestershire sauce, and dry mustard.

Cover and microwave on HIGH 100% power 4-6 minutes until the mushrooms are soft, stirring halfway through the cooking time.

Stir in the sour cream and shrimp. Cover and microwave on MEDIUM 50% power 3-5 minutes until heated through. Stir once during the cooking time.

Serve sprinkled with the reserved toasted almonds.

Note: If you are preparing the dish ahead, reheat on MEDIUM 50% power.

GREEN RICE

The colour and flavour of this quick, tasty, nutritious dish is a perfect complement to Sour Cream Shrimp Curry. It can be made ahead and reheated to serve.

4 tbsp.	oil	60 mL
2 cups	minced green onion	500 mL
2 cups	minced fresh parsley	500 mL
3 cups	finely chopped fresh spinach	750 mL
8 cups	chicken stock	2 L
4 cups	long-grain white rice	1 L
3 tsp.	salt	15 mL
1 tsp.	pepper	5 mL
	chopped red bell pepper for garnish	

Place the oil, green onion, parsley, and spinach in a large microproof casserole. Cover and microwave on HIGH 100% power 4-6 minutes until the vegetables are softened, stirring once during the cooking time.

Stir in the stock, rice, salt, and pepper. Cover and microwave on HIGH 100% power 20-25 minutes until the rice is softened. Stir at least once during the cooking time. Let stand, covered, for about 5 minutes to allow all the moisture to be absorbed.

Serve garnished with chopped red pepper.

MUSHROOMS OREGANO

Marinated ahead and heated through at serving time, these mushrooms are perfectly simple and perfectly delicious. Select tiny button mushrooms or cut larger ones in half.

3 lbs.	fresh mushrooms	1.5 kg
1/2 cup	olive oil	125 mL
1 tbsp.	lemon juice	15 mL
2	cloves garlic, minced	2
2 tsp.	salt	10 mL
1 tsp.	black pepper	5 mL
4 tbsp.	chopped fresh oregano, or	60 mL
2 tbsp.	dried oregano	30 mL

Trim the stems from the mushrooms. Wash, dry on a paper towel, and place in a shallow dish.

Beat the remaining ingredients together and pour over the mushrooms. Cover and marinate for at least 2 hours, stirring the marinade over the mushrooms halfway through this time.

Drain the mushrooms. Thread them on wooden toothpicks, 2 or 3 mushrooms on each, and arrange in a shallow microproof dish.

Cover with plastic wrap, venting at one corner. Microwave on HIGH 100% power 8-10 minutes until the mushrooms are tender-crisp. Rearrange halfway through the cooking time. Serve hot.

HRISTMAS BRUNCH

This brunch menu is rich with the bright colours and heady flavours of the winter holiday season. Decorate the table with reds and greens to complement the colours of the dishes, then welcome your guests and let this hearty menu do the rest. Serves 8.

Hot Cranberry Orange Punch   *Fresh vegetable crudités*
Spinach and Red Pepper   *Buttered toast fingers*
  Wedges
Potted Turkey
Casserole Carbonora
Grasshopper Pie

HOT CRANBERRY ORANGE PUNCH

Served warm and mellow with cranberry, orange, and holiday spices, this is the ideal Christmas drink. A little rum or brandy stirred in just before serving will give that extra punch!

2 cups	water	500 mL
1/2 cup	sugar	125 mL
2	cinnamon sticks, each 2-3 inches (5-7.5 cm) long	2
1 tsp.	ground ginger	5 mL
1/2 tsp.	ground cloves	2 mL
1/2 tsp.	ground allspice	2 mL
6 cups	cranberry juice	1.5 L
1	12 oz. (355 mL) can frozen orange juice	1
1/2 cup	lemon juice	125 mL
	whole cloves and fresh orange slices for garnish	

Place the water and sugar in a large microproof jug or dish. Microwave on HIGH 100% power to bring to a boil. Stir to dissolve the sugar and add the spices. Microwave on HIGH 100% power to bring to a boil, then boil 5 minutes. Stir in the juices. Return to the microwave and heat on MEDIUM 50% power 10 minutes. If you are using a probe, program to 160°F on MEDIUM 50% power.

Stick whole cloves into the edges of the orange slices and serve the punch warm with the studded orange slices floating on top.

SPINACH AND RED PEPPER WEDGES

Delightfully seasonal in colour, this dish makes an appealing addition to the holiday brunch table. Cut it in wedges and serve it with fresh vegetable crudités.

1	16 oz. (450 g) round loaf sourdough bread	1
1	10 1/2 oz. (300 g) pkg. frozen chopped spinach	1
1 cup	sour cream	250 mL
1/2 cup	mayonnaise	125 mL
1	1 1/2 oz. (45 g) pkg. vegetable soup mix	1
1	large red bell pepper, seeded and finely chopped	1
1	8 oz. (250 mL) can water chestnuts, drained and chopped	1
2	green onions, finely chopped	2
1/4 tsp.	ground nutmeg	1 mL

Cut the top off the bread. Hollow out the loaf, leaving the crust intact to form a container.

Place the package of frozen spinach in the microwave. Microwave on HIGH 100% power 2 minutes. Remove the spinach from the package and place in a microproof bowl. Cover and microwave on HIGH 100% power 2-4 minutes longer until the spinach is cooked. Place in a colander and press firmly to remove all excess moisture. Set aside to cool completely.

Mix the cooled spinach with the sour cream, mayonnaise, and vegetable soup mix. Stir in about one-third of the chopped red pepper. Stir in the remaining ingredients. Chill until serving time.

To serve, spoon the spinach mixture into the hollowed-out bread. With the remaining chopped red pepper, arrange a wreath shape around the outside of the bread. Cut into wedges and serve.

POTTED TURKEY

Here is a recipe for a lovely holiday meat spread that will keep in the refrigerator for several days, ready to serve at a moment's notice with hot buttered toast fingers or crackers.

1 lb.	cooked turkey	500 g
4 oz.	cooked ham	125 g
1/2 tsp.	dried marjoram	2 mL
1/2 tsp.	dried thyme	2 mL
pinch	dried mace	pinch
1/2 tsp.	salt	2 mL
1/2 tsp.	black pepper	2 mL
1/2 cup	butter	125 mL

Finely mince the turkey and ham. Toss with the herbs, salt, and pepper. Place in a microproof dish. Add 4 tbsp. (60 mL) of the butter. Microwave on MEDIUM 50% power for 5 minutes, stirring twice during the cooking time. Pack into a crock or dish. Cool.

Place the remaining butter in a microproof measure. Microwave on MEDIUM 50% power until foaming. Let stand until the sediments sink to the bottom. Carefully pour the clear top layer of melted butter over the meat, making sure the entire surface and the edges are covered with butter. Refrigerate until set before serving.

CASSEROLE CARBONORA

This gorgeous dish looks great and is full of the flavours and fragrances of Italy. Best of all, it can be cooked and assembled ahead, ready for last-minute cooking at serving time.

1 lb.	potatoes	500 g
1/2 lb.	mushrooms, sliced	250 g
1/2	green bell pepper, seeded and chopped	1/2
1/2	red bell pepper, seeded and chopped	1/2
4 tbsp.	chopped onion	60 mL
3	eggs	3
1/4 tsp.	seasoning salt	1 mL
1/4 tsp.	white pepper	1 mL
1 1/2 cups	half-and-half cream	375 mL
1/2 lb.	bacon, chopped	250 g
2	large tomatoes, peeled, seeded, and sliced	2

Peel the potatoes and cut into even-sized pieces. Place in a microproof dish, cover, and microwave on HIGH 100% power 8-10 minutes until cooked, stirring halfway through the cooking time. Let stand, covered, for about 5 minutes, then slice.

Place the mushrooms, green and red peppers, and onion in a microproof dish. Cover and microwave on HIGH 100% power 3-5 minutes until the vegetables are soft, stirring once during the cooking time. Drain off excess moisture.

Beat together the eggs, salt, pepper, and cream.

Place the chopped bacon on a microproof bacon rack. Cover with a paper towel and microwave on HIGH 100% power 8-10 minutes until the bacon is cooked, rearranging halfway through the cooking time. Divide into 2 portions.

Place the sliced cooked potatoes in one layer in a 9 inch (23 cm) round microproof quiche dish or a 1 1/2 inch (7.5 cm) deep pie plate. Cover with a layer of the cooked vegetable mixture, 1 portion of the bacon and a layer of tomatoes.

Pour the beaten egg mixture over the vegetables. Cover with waxed paper and microwave on MEDIUM HIGH 70% power 20 minutes. Uncover and sprinkle with the remaining half of the cooked bacon. Microwave on

MEDIUM HIGH 70% power 10 minutes longer, until the mixture is barely set in the centre.

Let stand, covered, for about 5 minutes. Serve warm, cut into wedges.

GRASSHOPPER PIE

This is a pie that was made for the Christmas season! Soft and creamy, with a subtle green colour and the rich flavours of cream and peppermint, it is a snap to prepare in the microwave.

4 tbsp.	butter	60 mL
1 1/4 cups	chocolate cookie crumbs	300 mL
3 tbsp.	sugar	45 mL
4 tbsp.	ground or finely chopped almonds	60 mL
1	10 oz. (280 g) pkg. large marshmallows	1
1/2 cup	milk	125 mL
1 cup	whipping cream	250 mL
4 tbsp.	green crème de menthe,	60 mL
	or	
1 tsp.	peppermint essence, mixed with	5 mL
few drops	green food colouring	few drops
	whipped cream for garnish	
	miniature candy canes for garnish	

Place the butter in a 9 inch (23 cm) microproof pie plate. Microwave on HIGH 100% power 30-40 seconds until the butter is melted.

Stir in the cookie crumbs, sugar, and almonds. Press firmly and evenly into the bottom and sides of the pie plate. Microwave on HIGH 100% power 2 minutes. Cool.

Place the marshmallows and milk in a microproof casserole. Cover and microwave on HIGH 100% power 2-3 minutes until the mixture can be stirred smooth. Chill completely until thickened, stirring occasionally. Whip the cream and fold into the chilled marshmallow mixture. Fold in the crème de menthe.

Pour into the prepared pie shell. Chill several hours. At serving time, the shell is easily released from the pie plate if it is set for a few minutes on a hot dampened towel. Serve the pie decorated with swirls of whipped cream topped with miniature candy canes.

CASUAL APPETIZERS

Luscious light fare is just the ticket for some occasions. Try the elegant Sundown Buffet, the light but filling Winter Warm-Up, or the perfectly satisfying Old-Fashioned Scottish Tea, all guaranteed to help special events become fond memories!

CENTRE-ICE PUB PARTY

This hearty, savoury, pub-style feast is made to order for that great Canadian sport—watching the hockey game. Add some easy and delicious deli pastries to these finger-food recipes—then fill a big tub with ice and cold drinks, invite the gang over, and have fun! Serves 8.

Angels on Horseback
Potted Cheddar
Curried Stuffed Eggs
Spicy Honey-Glazed Prawns
Savoury Crab-Stuffed
   Mushrooms

Cornish pasties, sausage rolls,
   ham and cheese rolls, beef
   pies, chicken pies, pork pies,
   Scotch pies
Assorted crackers
Assorted mustards and sauces

ANGELS ON HORSEBACK

Serve these popular savoury pub snacks sizzling hot from the broiler, arranged on a platter of crispy buttered toasts. Accompany with lemon wedges and shakers of malt vinegar and salt.

1 lb.	sliced bacon	500 g
32	fresh shucked oysters, clams, or a combination	32
16	slices bakery-style white bread, sliced 1/2 inch (1 cm) thick, crusts removed	16
1 cup	softened butter	250 mL
1 tsp.	bottled hot pepper sauce	5 mL
1/3 cup	finely minced fresh parsley	75 mL
	lemon wedges for garnish	
	shaker of malt vinegar	
	shaker of salt	

Cut each slice of bacon in half, making 32 slices. Wrap each oyster and/or clam in bacon, rolling up and securing with a wooden toothpick. Cut each slice of bread into quarters. Blend the butter and hot pepper sauce together, and spread on one side of each bread triangle. Heat the broiler.

Broil the buttered toasts 4-5 inches (10-12.5 cm) from the heat source until golden brown and crispy on top. Remove from the broiler and set aside on a wire rack.

Broil the bacon-wrapped shellfish 3 inches (7.5 cm) from the heat source on a rack, turning once, until very crispy and golden brown. Place each on a hot piece of toast. Sprinkle with parsley. Serve immediately, accompanied by the lemon wedges, vinegar, and salt.

The Easy Gourmet features a photograph of this recipe on page 53.

POTTED CHEDDAR

Serve this savoury potted cheddar with an assortment of crackers, crisps, and melba toasts. Let stand at room temperature 30 minutes before serving.

1 lb.	sharp cheddar cheese, shredded	500 g
1	8 oz. (250 g) pkg. cream cheese, softened	1
1/3 cup	finely minced green onion	75 mL
4 tbsp.	finely minced fresh parsley	60 mL
2 tbsp.	*each* dry sherry and mayonnaise	30 mL
1 tbsp.	prepared English-style mustard	15 mL
1 tbsp.	*each* packed brown sugar and Worcestershire sauce	15 mL
dash	cayenne pepper	dash
1/3 cup	chopped almonds, toasted in a 325°F (160°C) oven 8-10 minutes and cooled	75 mL

Beat together the grated cheddar and cream cheese until smooth. Add the green onion, parsley, sherry, mayonnaise, mustard, brown sugar, Worcestershire, and cayenne. Mix well. Pack into a wide-mouthed crock. Cover with the toasted almonds. Chill 24 hours. Bring to room temperature 30 minutes before serving in the crock surrounded by assorted crisp crackers.

The Easy Gourmet features a photograph of this recipe on page 53.

CURRIED STUFFED EGGS

An elegant blend of flavours gives an unusual touch to this casual but very festive dish.

8	hard-cooked eggs, chilled	8
1/3 cup	mayonnaise	75 mL
1 1/4 tsp.	curry powder	6 mL
1 tbsp.	chutney, minced	15 mL
2 tbsp.	sweet pickle relish	30 mL
2 tbsp.	minced green onion	30 mL
1 tsp.	dry English-style mustard	5 mL
2 tbsp.	tiny capers	30 mL
	salt and pepper to taste	
	minced fresh parsley and paprika for garnish	

Shell the eggs. Carefully cut each in half lengthwise. Remove the yolks and place in a small bowl. Mash the yolks with the back of a fork. Add the mayonnaise, curry powder, chutney, pickle relish, green onion, and mustard. Mix well until smooth. Stir in the capers, and season to taste with salt and pepper. Spoon the yolk mixture into the egg whites or pipe with a pastry bag fitted with a plain or star tip. Sprinkle the tops with a dusting of minced parsley and a sprinkling of paprika for colour. Chill several hours before serving.

The Easy Gourmet features a photograph of this recipe on page 53.

Opposite: Centre-Ice Pub Party (pp. 50-56)—(clockwise from right) Curried Stuffed Eggs, Spicy Honey-Glazed Prawns, Savoury Crab-Stuffed Mushrooms, Angels on Horseback, Potted Cheddar.

SPICY HONEY-GLAZED PRAWNS

Marinate these succulent prawns 30 minutes, pop them into the broiler, then serve sizzling hot on a wooden platter and watch them disappear.

1 cup	tomato-based chili sauce	250 mL
1/2 cup	honey	125 mL
1 tsp.	dry English-style mustard	5 mL
1 tbsp.	prepared horseradish	15 mL
4 tbsp.	vegetable oil	60 mL
1 tsp.	*each* dried thyme and chili powder	5 mL
2 1/2 lbs.	large or jumbo prawns, peeled and deveined, tails left intact	1.25 kg

Whisk together the chili sauce, honey, mustard, horseradish, oil, thyme, and chili powder. Toss the marinade with the prawns and let stand 30 minutes. Heat the broiler. Just before serving, broil the prawns in a single layer on a shallow foil-lined pan 2 inches (5 cm) from the heat, turning once. Cook 3-4 minutes or just until firmed and opaque, and slightly charred on the edges. Do not overcook. Serve hot or warm, mounded on a platter.

The Easy Gourmet features a photograph of this recipe on page 53.

SAVOURY CRAB-STUFFED MUSHROOMS

These marvellous treats can be prepared and assembled up to 24 hours ahead of time. Cover, chill, and at serving time, simply bake.

24	large fresh mushrooms with tightly closed caps, wiped clean with a damp cloth	24
8 tbsp.	butter	120 mL
1/3 cup	minced green onion (white and green parts)	75 mL
1/2 cup	fresh white bread crumbs	125 mL
2 tsp.	grated lemon rind	10 mL
2 tsp.	fresh lemon juice	10 mL
1	3 oz. (114 mL) jar minced pimientos, drained	1
1 cup	flaked crab meat or imitation crab meat	250 mL
1 tbsp.	*each* minced fresh dill and parsley	15 mL
1	egg, lightly beaten	1
1 cup	shredded Monterey jack or Swiss cheese	250 mL
1/4 cup	white wine or water	50 mL
	lemon wedges and minced fresh parsley or sprigs of dill for garnish	

Remove the mushroom stems, leaving cavities in the tops for stuffing. Finely chop the stems. Melt 4 tbsp. (60 mL) of the butter in a skillet over medium-high heat. Add the chopped stems and green onion. Sauté, stirring, 5-6 minutes until softened and pale golden. Remove from the heat and transfer the mixture to a mixing bowl. Let cool 15 minutes. Stir in the bread crumbs, lemon rind, lemon juice, pimientos, crab meat, the 1 tbsp. (15 mL) each dill and parsley, the egg, and the cheese. Toss lightly but thoroughly to combine. Set aside. Heat the remaining 4 tbsp. (60 mL) butter and turn the caps quickly in the butter to coat on both sides. Place the caps side by side in a 9 x 13 inch (23 x 33 cm) baking dish. Mound filling in the centre of each cap, pressing lightly to bind together. (The mushrooms may be prepared to this point, then covered and refrigerated up to 24 hours.)

Heat the oven to 400°F (200°C). Pour the wine into the bottom of the baking dish. Bake uncovered for 20 minutes, or until sizzling hot and bubbly. Let stand 10 minutes before serving. Serve on a platter accompanied by lemon wedges and a sprinkling of parsley or dill.

The Easy Gourmet features a photograph of this recipe on page 53.

ID-WINTER PARTY NIBBLES

This menu is a great excuse to gather everyone around for a terrific set of "nibbles." It is a casual party menu, guaranteed to take care of itself once it's on the table. Invite your guests to taste and sample, and offer the last of the seasonal sweets for the perfect finishing touch. Serves 8.

Herbed Currant Scones
Hot and Savoury Creamed
  Onion Soup
Pastry Cheese and Seed Straws
Old-Fashioned Gingerbread
  Men

Shaved roast turkey or ham
Assorted mustards, jams, and
  marmalades
Holiday nuts, candies, and
  fudge

HERBED CURRANT SCONES

These miniature currant and herb-studded scones are finger-food appetizers like no other. Just split and fill with thin shavings of leftover holiday roast turkey and ham, and set out crocks of mustards and jams. Makes 24 2 1/4 inch (5.6 cm) scones.

4 cups	all-purpose flour	1 L
2 tbsp.	sugar	30 mL
2 tsp.	baking powder	10 mL
1 tsp.	baking soda	5 mL
1 tsp.	salt	5 mL
1/2 cup	softened butter	125 mL
2 tbsp.	*each* fresh thyme leaves and minced fresh parsley	30 mL
1 tbsp.	minced fresh sage	15 mL
1 1/2 cups	whipping cream	375 mL
3/4 cup	dried currants, rinsed in warm water and drained	175 mL
	whipping cream for brushing	

Sift the dry ingredients together in a large mixing bowl. Cut in the butter with a pastry cutter (or use a food processor) until the mixture resembles coarse crumbs. Stir in the minced herbs and mix or process 1 minute. Add the cream and mix just until the dough holds together. Add the currants and mix gently to combine. Wrap the dough in plastic wrap and chill 2-3 hours or overnight.

Heat the oven to 375°F (190°C). Roll out the dough on a floured surface 3/4 inch (2 cm) thick. Cut out with a round or heart-shaped 2 inch (5 cm) cutter. Place the scones on lightly greased baking sheets, brush the tops with cream, and bake 12-15 minutes or until puffed and golden brown. Serve hot or warm.

HOT AND SAVOURY CREAMED ONION SOUP

A piping hot tureen of this silky, creamy, nourishing onion soup is just the ticket for a holiday get-together. Serve with crisp Pastry Cheese and Seed Straws (recipe follows) in a pretty basket.

1/2 lb.	bacon	250 g
1/2 cup	butter	125 mL
4 lbs.	large onions, halved and very thinly sliced	2 kg
4-6	cloves garlic, pressed	4-6
2 tbsp.	light brown sugar	30 mL
1 tsp.	*each* dried thyme and dill	5 mL
6 cups	chicken stock	1.5 L
2 cups	whipping cream	500 mL
1/4 cup	fresh lemon juice	50 mL
1/2 tsp.	bottled hot pepper sauce	2 mL
pinch	ground nutmeg	pinch
	salt and pepper to taste	
1/2 cup	minced fresh chives	125 mL

In a heavy stock pot sauté the bacon until crispy and golden brown. Remove with a slotted spoon and set aside to drain on absorbent paper.

Heat the butter with the bacon drippings over medium heat until sizzling. Add the onion and sauté, stirring, for 15 minutes. Add the garlic and brown sugar and sauté 15 minutes longer. The onions should be pale golden and softened. Add the thyme, dill, and chicken stock. Bring to a simmer, partially cover, and cook 30 minutes. Cool to barely warm.

In small batches, purée the soup to a creamy texture. Return it to the pot. Add the whipping cream, lemon juice, hot pepper sauce, and nutmeg. Bring to a simmer, and cook 25 minutes to heat through and thicken. Season to taste with salt and pepper. Set the soup aside until ready to serve. Reheat gently over low heat before serving.

Ladle into bowls or mugs, top with a sprinkling of crispy bacon and minced chives, and serve piping hot.

PASTRY CHEESE AND SEED STRAWS

The secret of these fabulous puff pastry straws is a small, simple package of ready-to-use frozen puff pastry. Makes 1 dozen each of 3 flavours.

1	14 oz. (400 g) pkg. frozen puff pastry, thawed	1
4 tbsp.	sesame seeds	60 mL
4 tbsp.	poppy seeds	60 mL
4 tbsp.	grated Parmesan cheese or finely grated cheddar cheese	60 mL

Divide the thawed pastry into thirds. Line 3 baking sheets with baking parchment. Heat the oven to 400°F (200°C).

On a lightly floured surface, roll out 1 piece of the pastry into a 10 x 10 inch (25 x 25 cm) square, 1/8 inch (3 mm) thick. Sprinkle the sesame seeds evenly over the pastry. Gently press them in by running a rolling pin over the top. With a pastry wheel or a zig-zag pastry wheel, cut strips 3/4 inch (2 cm) wide and 10 inches (25 cm) long. Gently twist each strip "barber pole" fashion as you place it on the baking sheet. Repeat with all strips. Bake 8-10 minutes until puffed and golden brown. Cool on the baking sheet 5 minutes, then transfer to wire racks.

Repeat the directions with another piece of pastry, using poppy seeds instead of sesame seeds, and prepare the third piece of pastry with grated cheese.

OLD-FASHIONED GINGERBREAD MEN

These deliciously spicy favourites are made with a dough sturdy enough for large 6 inch (15 cm) high cookies. Makes 3 dozen.

4 1/2 cups	unbleached flour	1125 mL
2 tsp.	*each* ground cinnamon, ginger, allspice, and nutmeg	10 mL
1 1/2 tsp.	baking soda	7 mL
1 tsp.	baking powder	5 mL
2 tsp.	salt	10 mL
1 cup	softened butter	250 mL
3/4 cup	brown sugar, packed	175 mL
2	eggs, at room temperature	2
1 tbsp.	finely grated orange rind	15 mL
1 1/2 cups	molasses	375 mL
	red hot candies, raisins, currants, and almonds for decoration	

Sift together the dry ingredients twice, and set aside. In a large mixer bowl, beat the butter and sugar until light and fluffy. Add the eggs one at a time, beating well after each addition, until very smooth. Add the flour mixture 1 cup (250 mL) at a time, beating after each addition until thoroughly combined. Stir in the orange rind and molasses and beat well. Divide the dough into thirds and flatten each third into a 1 inch (2.5 cm) thick round. Wrap in waxed paper and then in sealable plastic bags. Chill several hours, or up to 1 week.

Heat the oven to 375°F (190°C). Lightly grease baking sheets, or line with baking parchment. On a floured surface, roll each piece of dough to just over 1/8 inch (3 mm) thick. With a floured cookie cutter, cut out large gingerbread men. Transfer carefully (a metal spatula will help) to the prepared baking sheets. For a touch of whimsy, bend some figures slightly to create "action men." Press the red hot candies, raisins, currants, and almonds into the dough for eyes, mouth, and buttons if desired.

Bake 8-10 minutes until set and the edges just begin to colour a bit. Cool on the baking sheet 4 minutes, then, using a wide metal spatula, transfer them to wire racks to cool completely. Cool 1-2 hours to firm completely. Store in an airtight container to keep the cookies firm and crisp.

ANTIPASTO BUFFET

Here is an Italian-inspired hors d'oeuvres party that looks its best on your favourite rustic plates, platters, and baskets. Lay it all out around a centrepiece of fresh seasonal fruits, add a jug of breadsticks, and invite your guests to sample all of the distinctive pungent flavours of the Mediterranean. Buon appetito! Serves 6-8.

Sicilian Stuffed Mushrooms
Tomato and Basil Crostini
Eggplant Caponata

Prosciutto and melon
Assorted dry salami, mortadella,
*   Italian cheeses, and cured*
*   Mediterranean olives*
Italian breadsticks
Espresso coffee and amaretti
*   cookies*

SICILIAN STUFFED MUSHROOMS

These savoury, Italian-inspired stuffed mushrooms are just the thing for an appetizer buffet. They may be assembled up to 12 hours ahead of time, refrigerated, and heated 20 minutes in a hot oven before serving.

24	medium-large white mushrooms with firm, tightly-closed caps (choose uniform sizes), wiped clean with a damp cloth	24
1/2 lb.	Italian bulk sausage meat or Italian sausages with casings removed	250 g
1	small onion, minced	1
1	large clove garlic, minced	1
1/2 tsp.	dried oregano	2 mL
1 tsp.	finely grated lemon rind	5 mL
4 tbsp.	*each* dried currants, pine nuts, and minced fresh parsley	60 mL
1 cup	grated mozzarella cheese	250 mL
4 tbsp.	olive oil	60 mL
1/3 cup	freshly grated Parmesan cheese	75 mL

Using a small, sharp knife, remove the mushroom stems, leaving each cap with a smooth, round cavity to stuff. Set the caps aside and mince the stems.

In a skillet, sauté the sausage meat over medium-high heat until crumbly and no longer pink. Add the minced mushroom stems, onion, and garlic. Sauté, stirring, until pale golden. Stir in the oregano, lemon rind, currants, pine nuts, and parsley, and simmer 5 minutes until the currants are plumped. Remove from the heat and cool 30 minutes. Stir in the mozzarella.

Lightly brush each mushroom cap with olive oil. Fill each cavity with 1 rounded tbsp. (15 mL) sausage filling. Arrange the caps in a close single layer in a shallow baking dish. Sprinkle the tops lightly with the Parmesan cheese. The dish may be covered at this point and refrigerated up to 12 hours.

Heat the oven to 400°F (200°C). Bake the mushrooms about 20 minutes, or until the mushrooms sizzle and the filling is bubbly. Serve hot or warm.

The Easy Gourmet features a photograph of this recipe on page 71.

TOMATO AND BASIL CROSTINI

Tomato and basil are natural go-togethers, and these little delicacies prove it! The spread and toasted breads may be prepared 24 hours in advance, and assembled quickly right before baking a brief 10 minutes in the oven.

4 tbsp.	butter	60 mL
1/2 cup	olive oil	125 mL
24	diagonal slices French or sourdough baguette, 2 inches (5 cm) in diameter and 1/2 inch (1 cm) thick (1 long loaf)	24
1/2 cup	finely chopped green onion	125 mL
3	cloves garlic, pressed	3
2 cups	chopped, seeded Roma tomatoes, about 2 lbs. (1 kg)	500 mL
1 tbsp.	*each* sugar and red wine vinegar	15 mL
2 tbsp.	tiny capers, drained	30 mL
1/4 tsp.	dried red pepper flakes	1 mL
1/3 cup	fresh basil leaves, stacked and cut into thin julienne	75 mL
6	slices bacon, fried crisp and crumbled	6
	cracked black pepper to taste	

Heat the oven to 325°F (160°C). Melt the butter and 1/4 cup (50 mL) of the olive oil together. Brush lightly over both sides of the bread slices. Bake on a shallow baking sheet 10-15 minutes, turning once, until pale golden and crisp. Remove and set aside.

Heat the remaining 1/4 cup (50 mL) olive oil in a large skillet. Add the green onion and garlic and sauté, stirring, until softened and pale golden. Add the tomatoes, increase the heat to high, and sauté until the tomatoes release and then reabsorb their juices. The mixture should be thick and pulpy. Stir in the sugar, vinegar, capers, and red pepper flakes. Heat 5 minutes until bubbly, remove from the heat, and cool to room temperature. Stir in the julienned basil when the mixture is cooled.

To assemble the crostini, heat the oven to 350°F (180°C). Spread the tomato mixture over the tops of the toasted breads, leaving a 1/8 inch (6 mm) border all around. Sprinkle the tops with crumbled bacon. Bake 10-12 minutes, or until the filling is hot and bubbly. Serve hot or warm. Sprinkle with cracked black pepper to taste.

The Easy Gourmet features a photograph of this recipe on page 71.

EGGPLANT CAPONATA

Caponata is a Sicilian specialty—a sort of stewed fresh vegetable appetizer-relish. Prepare it several days ahead—it will just get better and better.

1 cup	olive oil	250 mL
2	eggplants, cut into 1/2 inch (1 cm) dice	2
2	zucchini, cut into 1/2 inch (1 cm) dice	2
1	*each* red, green, and yellow bell pepper, cut into 1/2 inch (1 cm) dice	1
2	medium-large onions, diced	2
10	stalks celery, sliced crosswise 1/4 inch (6 mm) thick	10
8	Roma tomatoes, cut into 1/2 inch (1 cm) dice	8
3 tbsp.	sugar	45 mL
1/3 cup	red wine vinegar	75 mL
1/3 cup	drained capers	75 mL
2/3 cup	minced fresh parsley	150 mL
2/3 cup	tiny Mediterranean cured black olives	150 mL
1 tsp.	*each* dried oregano, thyme, and basil	5 mL
1/2 tsp.	salt	2 mL
	cracked black pepper to taste	

Heat 1/2 cup (125 mL) of the olive oil in a very large skillet over medium-high heat. Add the eggplant and sauté, stirring, until softened and pale golden. Remove with a slotted spoon and set aside. Heat the remaining 1/2 cup (125 mL) olive oil and add the zucchini, peppers, onion, and celery. Sauté over high heat, stirring quickly, just until the edges are golden brown.

Return the eggplant to the skillet, toss with the other vegetables, and add the tomatoes. Cook over high heat until the tomatoes lose and then reabsorb their juices, about 5-6 minutes. Add the sugar, vinegar, and capers and cook 4-5 minutes, or until bubbly and thickened. Stir in 1/3 cup (75 mL) of the parsley, the olives, oregano, thyme, basil, salt, and pepper. Heat through 15 minutes, stirring several times. Taste and correct for seasonings. Cool to room temperature. Transfer to a large crockery bowl or glass jars, cover tightly, and refrigerate up to 3 days.

To serve, mound the chilled caponata in a large, rustic bowl, and sprinkle with the remaining 1/3 cup (75 mL) parsley.

The Easy Gourmet features a photo of this recipe on page 71.

GREEK APPETIZER PARTY

Most of the recipes in this appetizer buffet, rich and fragrant with the classic flavours of Greece, can be prepared ahead and quickly baked or fried before serving. Serve on a wooden table with a hand-woven runner, colourful cotton napkins, and heavy hand-blown glasses for cool beverages. To coin a phrase, "When in Greece...enjoy!" Serves 8.

Melitzanosalata	*Warm or toasted pita breads*
Savoury Greek Meatballs	*Greek kalamata olives*
Tzatziki Sauce	*Feta cheese squares drizzled with olive oil*

MELITZANOSALATA

Serve this wonderful Greek eggplant dip surrounded by warm pita bread or buttered and broiled pita bread triangles. Serve cool for the best flavour. Makes 2 1/2 cups (625 mL).

1	1 1/2 lb. (750 g) eggplant	1
	olive oil to coat	
1 tsp.	salt	5 mL
2	large cloves garlic, minced	2
1/2 cup	fresh white bread crumbs	125 mL
3 tbsp.	fresh lemon juice	45 mL
1/2 cup	olive oil	125 mL
1	small onion, minced	1
2	small, firm, ripe tomatoes, seeded and finely diced	2
1/3 cup + 2 tbsp.	minced fresh parsley	105 mL
	freshly ground black pepper to taste	

Heat the oven to 400°F (200°C). Rub the eggplant all over with a light film of olive oil. Place on a baking sheet, pierce the skin in several places, and bake until very soft, about 1 hour. Cool to room temperature, and then split in half. Scoop out all of the cooked flesh. From this point, work quickly so that the eggplant does not discolour.

In a food processor fitted with a steel blade, process the salt and garlic to a fine paste. Add the eggplant pulp and process to a coarse purée. Add the bread crumbs and lemon juice. With the motor running, add the olive oil in a thin, steady stream. Transfer the mixture to a bowl. Stir in the onion, tomato, and 1/3 cup (75 mL) of the minced parsley. Season with pepper to taste. Cover and chill 6 hours or overnight. Serve chilled or cool, sprinkled with the remaining 2 tbsp. (30 mL) parsley.

SAVOURY GREEK MEATBALLS

Serve these succulent Greek-flavoured meatballs accompanied by the tangy, cold Tzatziki Sauce.

2 tbsp.	butter	30 mL
1	large onion, minced	1
2 tbsp.	dried mint, crumbled	30 mL
2	eggs, beaten	2
1 cup	fresh white bread crumbs	250 mL
4 tbsp.	freshly grated Parmesan cheese	60 mL
1/3 cup	minced fresh parsley	75 mL
2 tbsp.	fresh lemon juice	30 mL
	grated rind of 1 lemon (yellow part only)	
2 lbs.	lean ground lamb	1 kg
2 tsp.	salt	10 mL
1/2 tsp.	*each* black pepper and ground cinnamon	2 mL
	flour for coating	
	vegetable oil for frying	
	Tzatziki Sauce (recipe follows)	

Heat the butter in a skillet. Add the minced onion and sauté until softened and pale golden on the edges. Stir in the mint, sauté 2 minutes, and set the skillet aside to cool to room temperature. Meanwhile, combine the eggs, bread crumbs, Parmesan cheese, parsley, lemon juice, and lemon rind and let stand 20 minutes.

In a large mixing bowl, combine the lamb, salt, onion-mint mixture, and egg mixture, pepper, and cinnamon. Mix thoroughly. Knead gently with your hands or an electric mixer fitted with a dough hook. Cover and refrigerate 2 hours or overnight.

With moistened hands, form 32 round meatballs, each 1 1/4 inches (3 cm) in diameter. Roll each lightly in flour to coat. Heat vegetable oil in a deep skillet to a depth of 3 inches (7.5 cm), to a temperature of 375°F (190°C). (The frying temperature is right when a bit of bread dropped in rises to the top immediately and begins to sizzle.) Fry the meatballs in small batches, turning until golden brown on all sides, 5-6 minutes. Remove from the pan with a mesh strainer and drain on absorbent paper.

Serve the warm meatballs on a platter with a bowl of chilled Tzatziki Sauce on the side, for dipping.

TZATZIKI SAUCE

Makes 2 1/2 cups (625 mL).

1/2	long English cucumber (or 2 small cucumbers), peeled and seeded	1/2
	salt for sprinkling	
2 cups	plain yogurt	500 mL
2 tsp.	white vinegar	10 mL
2	small cloves garlic, pressed	2
1 tbsp.	*each* minced fresh dill and fresh mint, or to taste	15 mL
	salt and white pepper to taste	

Grate the cucumber. Place in a colander and sprinkle lightly with salt. Let stand 30 minutes to pull out the excess water. Rinse and press dry between layers of towel. Whisk the yogurt smooth. Stir in the vinegar, grated cucumber, garlic, dill, and mint. Season to taste with salt and white pepper. Cover and chill several hours. Serve chilled.

SUNDOWN BUFFET

Designed for an informal late afternoon gathering, this menu features light, scrumptious, great-looking party foods. Check the deli department for special cocktail sauces and the meat department for frozen seafood hors d'oeuvres, then give star billing to the Party Sandwich Loaf. Serves 12.

Mini Gougères   *Seafood hors d'oeuvres*
Tiny Tourtières   *Assorted cocktail sauces*
Party Sandwich Loaf

MINI GOUGÈRES

Puffy and golden brown, and fragrant with herbs and cheese, these bite-sized morsels have a tendency to disappear quickly, so make plenty!

1 cup	water	250 mL
4 tbsp.	butter	60 mL
1 cup	all-purpose flour	250 mL
2	eggs	2
1/2 cup	chopped cooked shrimp	125 mL
1 tsp.	Dijon mustard	5 mL
1/2 cup	grated Swiss cheese	125 mL
1	clove garlic, chopped	1
1 tsp.	chopped fresh parsley	5 mL
1/2 tsp.	dried oregano	2 mL
1/2 tsp.	dried savoury	2 mL

Heat the oven to 400°F (200°C). Grease 2 baking sheets and set aside.

In a medium saucepan, combine the water and butter and bring to a boil. Remove from the heat and stir in the flour until the mixture pulls away from the sides of the pan and forms a slight skin on the bottom. Return to the heat and cook 1 minute, stirring constantly.

Transfer to a medium bowl or food processor and add the eggs one at a time, beating well after each addition. Blend in the shrimp along with the remaining ingredients.

Drop the batter by teaspoonfuls onto the baking sheets. Bake 25-30 minutes or until puffed and very well browned.

Remove from the oven and pierce each puff with a toothpick to allow steam to escape. Serve hot.

To freeze, cool to room temperature and freeze on a baking sheet. Transfer to sealable plastic bags. Reheat, unthawed, 10-15 minutes at 325°F (180°C).

TINY TOURTIÈRES

Frozen puff pastry saves a step in the preparation of these popular hors d'oeuvres, inspired by the traditional French Canadian tourtière. Simply wonderful dipped in sour cream.

1 lb.	mixed ground veal, pork, and beef	500 g
1/2 cup	chicken stock	125 mL
1	medium onion, finely chopped	1
1	clove garlic, minced	1
1/2 tsp.	*each* dried thyme, sage, and dry mustard	2 mL
pinch	salt	pinch
1	medium potato, cooked and mashed	1
3	7 1/2 oz. (215 g) pkgs. frozen puff pastry, thawed	3
1	egg	1
1 tsp.	water	5 mL

In a large skillet, combine the meat, stock, onion, garlic, and seasonings. Heat to boiling. Reduce the heat and simmer, uncovered, 25 minutes or until most of the liquid is gone. Stir occasionally. Remove from the heat. Stir in the mashed potato. Taste for seasonings. Cool. On a floured surface, roll out the thawed puff pastry into a 12 inch (30 cm) square about 1/8 inch (6 mm) thick. Cut into 3 inch (7.5 cm) squares. Place about 1 tsp. (5 mL) of cooled meat mixture slightly off centre in each square. Fold over to form a triangle. Press the edges together well. The dish may be made ahead to this point and frozen.

Heat the oven to 375°F (190°C). Place the pastries on an ungreased baking sheet. Beat the egg with the water and brush over the tops. Bake 15-20 minues (30-40 minutes, if frozen) or until golden.

PARTY SANDWICH LOAF

Have time to enjoy your own party with this colourful make-ahead loaf. It may be refrigerated up to 2 days. Frost the loaf only after it is well chilled. For easier handling, cut each slice in half.

1	loaf unsliced sandwich bread	1
1/2 cup	softened butter	125 mL
3	sandwich fillings (recipes follow)	3
	Cream Cheese Icing (recipe follows)	
	radishes, parsley, nuts, olives, and/or pickles	
	for garnish	

Carefully trim the crusts from the bread and cut the loaf into 4 lengthwise slices of equal thickness. Butter the first slice and spread with one filling. Butter both sides of the second slice, place it on top of the filling, and spread with the second filling. Repeat with the third slice and third filling. Butter the last slice on one side and place on top.

Refrigerate the loaf for 1-24 hours, well wrapped. Then ice the top and sides with Cream Cheese Icing. Chill until serving time. To serve, place the loaf on a rectangular platter. Garnish as desired. Cut into 1 inch (2.5 cm) slices.

CREAM CHEESE ICING

2	8 oz. (250 g) pkgs. cream cheese	2
1/3 cup	milk	75 mL

Blend the cream cheese with enough milk to spread easily.

Opposite: Antipasto Buffet (pp. 61-64) and selections from Winter Warm-up (pp. 74-77) and Contemporary Mini-Feast (pp. 78-82)—(counter-clockwise from top left) Spicy Bacon-Cheese Twists, Beefy Cheese Log, Sicilian Stuffed Mushrooms, Tomato and Basil Crostini, Pizza Rounds, Eggplant Caponata.

CHICKEN FILLING

2/3 cup	minced cooked chicken	150 mL
2 tbsp.	chopped stuffed olives	30 mL
	mayonnaise to moisten	

Blend together the chicken and olives with enough mayonnaise to spread easily.

EGG FILLING

3	hard-cooked eggs, chopped	3
1 tsp.	prepared mustard	5 mL
	salt and pepper to taste	
	mayonnaise to moisten	

Prepare as above.

TUNA OR SALMON FILLING

2/3 cup	canned tuna or salmon	150 mL
2 tbsp.	pickle relish	30 mL
	mayonnaise to moisten	

Prepare as above.

SHRIMP FILLING

1/2 cup	cooked shrimp, chopped	125 mL
1	hard-cooked egg, chopped	1
2 tbsp.	minced celery	30 mL
	salt and pepper to taste	
	mayonnaise to moisten	

Prepare as above.

WINTER WARM-UP

After skiing (or skating, biking, or jogging), your friends are ready to eat!
Bring them in out of the cold for this nourishing, tasty mini-meal. This menu,
with its easy recipes that take advantage of refrigerator biscuits, mini pitas
from the deli, and make-ahead goodies, is designed for the cook who also
wants to join in the fun. Serves 8.

Pizza Rounds
Mini Pitas with Hummus
Hot Spinach Dip
Beefy Cheese Log

Fresh warmed baguettes with
  butter
Cheese sticks and assorted
  crackers

PIZZA ROUNDS

Quickly prepared after a busy day skiing or biking, these little treats are made
from convenient ingredients you can pick up on your way home.

1	pkg. refrigerator butterflake rolls	1
1 cup	pizza or spaghetti sauce	250 mL
1	large stick pepperoni, sliced	1
6	mushrooms, sliced	6
1	small green bell pepper, sliced	1
	grated mozzarella cheese	

Heat the oven to 400°F (200°C). Break open the butterflake rolls and pull
apart the segments. Press flat on a lightly greased baking sheet. Divide the
sauce among the rolls. Divide the sliced pepperoni, mushrooms, and green
pepper among the rolls. Sprinkle on the cheese.

Bake 10-12 minutes or until the rolls are browned, the cheese is melted, and
the sauce is bubbling. Serve at once.

The Easy Gourmet features a photograph of this recipe on page 71.

MINI PITAS WITH HUMMUS

Hors d'oeuvres size pitas are perfect for parties. In this recipe they are served with hummus, a traditional dip from the middle East. Makes about 2 cups (500 mL).

2	cloves garlic	2
1	19 oz. (540 mL) can chick peas, well drained	1
3 tbsp.	tahini (sesame butter) or creamy peanut butter	45 mL
2 tbsp.	chopped fresh parsley	30 mL
2 tbsp.	chopped fresh mint	30 mL
pinch	cayenne pepper	pinch
1-1 1/2 cups	olive oil	250-375 mL
8	hors d'oeuvres size pitas	8

Peel the garlic. With the food processor running, drop in the garlic and process until well minced. Add the chick peas and process to a rough purée. Add the tahini, parsley, and mint. Taste for seasonings and add cayenne pepper to taste.

With the machine running, pour in the olive oil in a thin, steady stream until the mixture becomes creamy. Chill several hours. Serve at room temperature.

Slice the mini pitas in half and spoon a little of the hummus into each. Arrange on a serving platter.

HOT SPINACH DIP

Serve this unusual hot dip with torn pieces of fresh baguette or rye crackers and crisp raw slivers of turnip, radishes, carrot, endive, or any of your favourites. Makes 6 cups (1.5 L).

2 cups	sour cream	500 mL
1 cup	mayonnaise	250 mL
1	3 oz. (77 g) pkg. dry leek soup mix	1
1	10 oz. (300 g) pkg. frozen chopped spinach, thawed and squeezed dry	1
1/2 cup	chopped fresh parsley	125 mL
1/2 cup	chopped green onion	125 mL
1 tsp.	dried dill	5 mL
1 tsp.	dried oregano	5 mL

Combine all ingredients in a medium saucepan. Gently heat until barely bubbling. Do not boil or the sour cream will curdle. Serve warm.

BEEFY CHEESE LOG

In this recipe, the long-time favourite flavour combination of ground beef, cheese, and chiles is baked and sliced into a hearty appetizer for hearty appetites. Serve with tomato chutney and slices of baguette.

2	eggs	2
1/2-1 cup	dry bread crumbs	125-250 mL
1	8 oz. (227 mL) jar taco or spaghetti sauce	1
2 tbsp.	finely minced onion	30 mL
1 1/2 tsp.	dried oregano	7 mL
1 1/2 tsp.	chili powder	7 mL
1/2 tsp.	ground cumin	2 mL
2 1/2 cups	shredded cheddar cheese	625 mL
2	cloves garlic, minced	2
2 lbs.	lean ground beef	1 kg
9	thin slices Black Forest ham	9
3	4 oz. (114 mL) cans chopped chiles, drained	3
1	4 oz. (125 g) can chopped black olives	1

In a large bowl, beat the eggs and add 1/2 cup (125 mL) of the bread crumbs, 4 tbsp. (60 mL) of the taco sauce, and the onion. Let stand 5 minutes. Mix in the oregano, chili, cumin, 1 cup (250 mL) of the cheese, the garlic, and ground beef. Add more crumbs if necessary to make a dry mixture. On a large piece of foil or parchment, spread the meat mixture into an 18 x 10 inch (45 x 25 cm) rectangle. Cut the meat into 3 strips, 6 x 10 inches (15 x 25 cm) each, cutting through the paper as well.

In the centre of each rectangle, layer on 3 slices of the ham, 1 can each of the drained chiles, a third of the remaining cheeses and a third of the can of olives. Starting with the long side, tightly roll the rectangles into logs, dampening your hands for easier rolling. Pinch the seams and ends of the meat together. Remove the foil or paper.

Heat the oven to 350°F (180°C). Place the rolls on a large, foil-lined baking sheet with sides. Spoon the remaining taco sauce over top. Bake 45 minutes or until the meat is brown and firm to the touch and the sauce is puffy. Cool in the pan. Drain. Wrap in foil and refrigerate 8 hours or up to 3 days. The meat logs can be frozen at this point.

Cut the chilled logs into thin slices and serve with rounds of bread.

The Easy Gourmet features a photograph of this recipe on page 71.

CONTEMPORARY MINI-FEAST

Here is a light, delicious, and very contemporary menu for the smaller, more intimate reception. Serve the breads and crackers in beribboned baskets, then let the elegant finger foods and spreads become the focus of the event. Make a special occasion even better with this extra-special buffet. Serves 16.

Shrimp-Mushroom Croustades
Salmon Cornucopias
Spicy Bacon-Cheese Twists
Tiny Cheese Balls
Savoury Mousse with Three
  Caviars
Crab Pâté

Deli antipasto with assorted
  crackers

SHRIMP-MUSHROOM CROUSTADES

A spicy filling topped with white cheddar cheese nestles in crisp bread cases—fast, easy, and perfectly addictive!

32	slices white bread	32
	butter to taste	
10	mushrooms, finely chopped	10
4 oz.	small cooked shrimp	125 g
1	10 oz. (284 mL) can golden mushroom soup	1
2-3 oz.	shredded white cheddar cheese	60-90 g

Heat the oven to 325°F (160°C). With a 2 1/2 inch (6 cm) cookie cutter or drinking glass, cut out 32 rounds of bread. Lightly butter one side of each round and press into muffin tins, buttered side down. Bake 15 minutes or until lightly browned. Let cool. The dish may be made ahead to this point.

Heat the broiler. Mix together the mushrooms, shrimp, and enough golden mushroom soup to bind the mixture together. Place the bread cases on a baking sheet and spoon in the mushroom mixture. Top with grated cheese.

Broil until bubbling, about 2 minutes. Serve at once.

SALMON CORNUCOPIAS

Finger foods that are delicious, lovely to look at, and easy to eat are the sign of a thoughtful hostess and the start of a great party. These salmon rolls fill the bill perfectly.

32	thin slices smoked salmon	32
1	8 oz. (250 g) pkg. cream cheese with green onion	1
2 tbsp.	chopped fresh parsley	30 mL
1	3 1/2 oz. (97 g) jar red caviar, or	1
1	3 1/2 oz. (100 g) jar red lumpfish caviar	1

Gently roll each slice of salmon into a tiny cornucopia. Place on waxed paper.

Cream the cheese until softened and stir in the parsley. Pipe into the centres of the smoked salmon rolls. Top each with a tiny dollop of red caviar. Chill until serving time.

SPICY BACON-CHEESE TWISTS

Frozen bread dough is the convenience secret of these delectable treats, baked to a golden turn with the flavours of cheese, bacon, and a touch of mustard. Makes 26.

1	loaf frozen bread dough, thawed	1
2 tsp.	melted butter	10 mL
3	slices bacon, cooked and crumbled	3
1/2 cup	grated cheddar cheese	125 mL
2 tbsp.	mayonnaise	30 mL
1 tsp.	dry mustard	5 mL

On a floured surface, roll out the bread dough as thin as possible into a rectangle. Brush with the butter.

Mix together the bacon, cheese, mayonnaise, and mustard. Spead this mixture over half the bread surface. Fold in half and press together. Cut into 2 x 1/2 inch (5 x 1 cm) strips. Twist each strip and place on a lightly greased baking sheet.

Bake at 375°F (190°C) for 12-15 minutes or until lightly browned.

The Easy Gourmet features a photograph of this recipe on page 71.

TINY CHEESE BALLS

Several tasty cheeses blend together in these dainty morsels. Roll some in nuts, some in parsley, and some in paprika, and serve with party toothpicks. Best of all, you can make them ahead, freeze them, and thaw them in the fridge.

1	8 oz. (250 g) pkg. pimiento cream cheese	1
1 cup	grated sharp cheddar cheese	250 mL
1/3 cup	grated Parmesan or Romano cheese	75 mL
1 tbsp.	prepared mustard	15 mL
1 tbsp.	chopped fresh parsley	15 mL
1/2 tsp.	cayenne pepper	2 mL
	chopped pecans and walnuts, chopped fresh parsley, and paprika for garnish	

Cream the cream cheese until it is soft. Stir in the other ingredients. Chill until firm enough to form balls.

Roll the cheese into balls about 1 inch (2.5 cm) in diameter. Roll in the various garnishes and chill until serving time.

SAVOURY MOUSSE WITH THREE CAVIARS

Three colourful caviars decorate the top of this tasty herbed mousse. The mousse can be made ahead, and the caviars added just before serving. Serve with thinly sliced dark rye bread.

1 cup	sour cream	250 mL
4 tbsp.	chopped fresh parsley	60 mL
4 tbsp.	mixed fresh chives, savoury,	60 mL
	and tarragon (or 1 tbsp. (15 mL) dried)	
1 tbsp.	fresh lemon juice	15 mL
1 tsp.	grated lemon rind	5 mL
1 tsp.	Worcestershire sauce	5 mL
1	envelope unflavoured gelatin	1
4 tbsp.	water	60 mL
1/2 cup	whipping cream, whipped	125 mL
	freshly ground black pepper	
	vegetable oil for coating pan	
2	2 oz. (50 g) jars whitefish golden caviar	2
1	3 1/2 oz. (100 g) jar black lumpfish caviar	1
1	2 oz. (57 g) jar red salmon caviar	1
	chopped green onion for garnish	

In a medium bowl, combine the sour cream, herbs, lemon juice, rind, and Worcestershire sauce.

In a small saucepan, sprinkle the gelatin over the water and let stand until soft, about 5 minutes. Place over low heat and cook, stirring, until completely dissolved, about 2 minutes. Stir into the sour cream mixture. Cool thoroughly, then fold in the whipped cream and pepper.

Line the bottom of an 8 inch (20 cm) springform pan with parchment or waxed paper and lightly coat with vegetable oil. Spoon the gelatin mixture into the pan and let stand several hours or overnight.

At serving time, carefully remove the mousse from the pan and place on a serving plate. Arrange the caviars in 1 inch (2.5 cm) rings around the mold, beginning with the red salmon in the middle, followed by a ring of yellow, followed by the black. Cover the remaining surface with chopped green onion.

CRAB PÂTÉ

Pâté makes any occasion special. This one is made with imitation crab, but use the real thing if you're going all out! Serve with melba rounds or crispy crackers. Makes about 2 cups (500 mL).

3	hard-cooked eggs	3
1/2 cup	butter	125 mL
1/2 cup	mayonnaise	125 mL
4 tbsp.	chopped fresh parsley	60 mL
2 tbsp.	chopped onion	30 mL
2 tbsp.	lemon juice	30 mL
1 tbsp.	Dijon mustard	15 mL
1	clove garlic, crushed	1
6 oz.	crab meat or imitation crab meat	180 g
	salt and pepper to taste	

Separate the eggs, reserving the whites. Place the yolks, butter, mayonnaise, parsley, onion, lemon juice, mustard, and garlic in the work bowl of a food processor or blender and purée until blended.

Finely chop the egg whites. Fold with the crab into the yolk mixture. Taste for seasonings and add salt and pepper to taste. Place in an attractive crock and refrigerate overnight to allow the flavours to mellow.

ROCK'N'ROLL BUFFET

Quick snacks are part of any teenager's day, so the microwave is perfect for a teen gathering. Easy enough for any young cook, but designed with just the right touch of grown-up sophistication, these wholesome and tasty recipes are guaranteed to get the ball rolling at any special event for the young adult set. Serves 8.

Curried Popcorn
Bacon-Onion Dip
Chili-Filled Individual Pita
  Breads
Microwave Nanaimo Bars

Fresh raw vegetables and
  assorted crackers
Fresh fruit platter

CURRIED POPCORN

The microwave makes perfect popcorn—light and fluffy, and this recipe is a delicious change-of-pace for a classic party snack. Use a microwave-designed popper and follow the manufacturer's directions.

For each 1/2 cup (125 mL) of unpopped corn:

1/2 cup	butter	125 mL
1 tsp.	curry powder	5 mL

Pop the corn according to manufacturer's directions for microwave popper. Turn into a large bowl.

Place the butter and curry powder in a microproof measure. Microwave on HIGH 100% power 40-60 seconds until the butter is melted. Stir and pour over the popped corn. Mix well and serve immediately.

BACON-ONION DIP

This is the favourite of all party-goers, teens and adults alike. Quick and easy to make, it tastes like you worked all day! Serve with fresh vegetable crudités and an assortment of crackers. Serves 8-10.

1/2 lb.	sliced bacon	250 g
1	1 1/2 oz. (42.5 g) pkg. onion soup mix	1
2 cups	sour cream	500 mL
	chopped green onion for garnish	

Place the bacon slices on a microproof bacon rack. Cover with a piece of paper towel and microwave on HIGH 100% power, allowing approximately 1 minute per slice, until the bacon is crisp. Rearrange the bacon twice during the cooking time. Let cool and crumble finely.

Mix the bacon, onion soup mix, and sour cream well. Pile into a serving bowl. Cover and refrigerate for at least 2 hours before serving. Top with chopped green onion, place on a large serving platter surrounded by crackers and/or fresh vegetable crudités, and serve.

CHILI-FILLED INDIVIDUAL PITA BREADS

These individual pita breads, filled with a meaty chili sauce and piled with an assortment of toppings, will appeal to any teenager. The microwave makes it easy for them to do it themselves. Serves 8.

8	hors d'oeuvre size pitas	8
1 lb.	ground beef	500 g
4 tbsp.	chopped green onion	60 mL
1 tbsp.	chili powder	15 mL
1 tsp.	dried oregano	5 mL
1/4 tsp.	garlic powder	1 mL
1 tsp.	salt	5 mL
	black pepper to taste	
1	14 oz. (398 mL) can Manwich tomato sauce	1
1	14 oz. (398 mL) can chili beans	1
	chopped green onion, grated cheddar cheese, shredded lettuce, chopped tomatoes, and sour cream for toppings	

Cut the top of each pita bread to open up the pockets. Wrap in a clean tea towel and set aside.

Crumble the beef into a microproof casserole. Microwave on MEDIUM 50% power 2-4 minutes until the meat is cooked. Stir well and drain off excess fat. Stir in the green onion, chili powder, oregano, garlic powder, salt, and pepper. Microwave on MEDIUM 50% power 2 minutes. Stir well.

Stir in the Manwich sauce and chili beans. Microwave on MEDIUM 50% power 5-8 minutes until heated through.

Place the pita breads, wrapped in a tea towel, in the microwave. Heat on HIGH 100% power 50 seconds to warm through.

To serve, fill each pita bread with chili. Place the toppings in bowls and let your guests help themselves.

MICROWAVE NANAIMO BARS

These irresistible treats can be made in minutes in the microwave. Serve them at any young people's gathering, and watch them disappear. Makes 16 squares.

Base

1/2 cup	butter	125 mL
4 tbsp.	sugar	60 mL
5 tbsp.	cocoa	75 mL
1 tsp.	vanilla	5 mL
1	egg	1
2 cups	graham cracker crumbs	500 mL
1 cup	fine dried coconut	250 mL
1/2 cup	chopped walnuts	125 mL

Filling

4 tbsp.	butter	60 mL
3 tbsp.	milk	45 mL
2 tbsp.	custard powder	30 mL
2 cups	sifted icing sugar	500 mL

Topping

2 oz.	semi-sweet chocolate	60 g
1 tbsp.	butter	15 mL

For the base, mix together the butter, sugar, cocoa, vanilla, and egg in a microproof bowl. Microwave on MEDIUM 50% power 2-3 minutes until the mixture resembles custard in consistency. Stir twice during the cooking time. Blend in the crumbs, coconut, and nuts. Press firmly and evenly into a 9 inch (23 cm) square pan.

For the filling, cream the butter with the milk, custard powder, and icing sugar until light and fluffy. Spread over the crumb base. Chill until set.

For the topping, place the chocolate and butter in a microproof measure. Microwave on MEDIUM 50% power 2-3 minutes until the chocolate is melted. Pour over the filling, tilting the pan until the chocolate coats the filling. Chill until set.

To serve, cut into squares.

HILDREN'S PIZZA PARTY

Making dinner is half the party fun in this menu for youngsters—the guests design their own pizzas, then they get to eat their own goofy creations. Planned with the maximum of fun to please the kids and nutrition to please the adults, this menu is the centrepiece of one great children's party. Serves 12.

Funny Face Pizzas   Fruit punch
Peanut Butter Crispy   Fresh vegetables with cheesy dip
  Squares

FUNNY FACE PIZZAS

Kids love to help create their own food—so let the party fun include the guests making their own pizzas. Ingredients for making the "faces" can vary: try olives, carrot pieces, or fresh fruit as well as these suggestions.

6	English muffins, split and toasted	6
1	14 oz. (395 mL) jar pizza sauce	1
12	slices pepperoni sausage, 3 inches (7.5 cm)in diameter	12
12	slices mozzarella cheese	12
24	slices pepperoni sausage, 1/4 inch (6 mm) in diameter	24
6	pineapple chunks, halved lengthwise	6
6	gherkin pickles, halved lengthwise	6

Spread the English muffin halves with pizza sauce. Top each with a slice of 3 inch (7.5 cm) pepperoni. Top each with a slice of mozzarella cheese.

With the smaller pepperoni sausage, fashion eyes on each half. Use half a pineapple chunk for the nose and half a gherkin pickle for the mouth.

Arrange the pizzas in a circle in the microwave. Microwave on MEDIUM 50% power 2-4 minutes until the cheese is melted.

Serve immediately.

PEANUT BUTTER CRISPY SQUARES

These are guaranteed to be a hit at any kids' party. They freeze well, so make them ahead for maximum convenience and let them thaw before serving.

Base

1/2 cup	brown sugar	125 mL
1 cup	crunchy peanut butter	250 mL
1/2 cup	light corn syrup	125 mL
2 tsp.	butter	10 mL
2 cups	crispy rice cereal	500 mL
1 cup	corn flakes	250 mL

Topping

1 cup	brown sugar	250 mL
2 tbsp.	milk or cream	30 mL
2 tbsp.	light corn syrup	30 mL
1 tsp.	vanilla	5 mL
2-3 cups	sifted icing sugar	500-750 mL

For the base, place the brown sugar, peanut butter, corn syrup, and butter in a large microproof dish. Microwave on MEDIUM 50% power 2-4 minutes until dissolved. Stir well and blend in the crispy rice cereal and corn flakes, taking care not to crush the cereal. Spread evenly into an 8 inch (20 cm) square pan.

For the topping, place the brown sugar, milk, and corn syrup in a microproof dish. Microwave on MEDIUM 50% power until dissolved. Stir well and microwave on HIGH 100% power to bring to a boil. Stir in the vanilla. Blend in the icing sugar just until a soft spreading consistency is reached. Spread evenly over the prepared base. Chill until set and cut into squares.

Opposite: Selections from Traditional Christmas Dinner (pages 100-104)—(clockwise from top) Turkey with All the Trimmings, Steamed Pudding with Orange Brandy Sauce, Brussels Sprouts with Buttered Crumbs.

OLD-FASHIONED SCOTTISH TEA

Nothing warms up a winter afternoon like a comforting tea served by a blazing fire. For this traditional Scottish tea, your prettiest china and your best friends are all you have to add to an assortment of fresh-from-the-oven delicacies. Serves 10-12.

Pitcaithly Bannock
Scottish Fruit Griddle Scones
Dundee Cake

PITCAITHLY BANNOCK

Similar to the well-known buttery Scottish shortbread, this treat is delicately sweet and buttery, with a snap of citrus flavour and the crunch of almonds. Makes 16 wedges.

1 1/3 cups	all-purpose flour	325 mL
3 tbsp.	rice flour	45 mL
3/4 cup	butter, at room temperature	175 mL
1/3 cup	sugar	75 mL
2 tbsp.	finely chopped mixed cut citrus peel	30 mL
4 tbsp.	finely chopped blanched almonds	60 mL
	sugar for sprinkling	

Heat the oven to 325°F (160°C).

In a mixing bowl, place the flour and rice flour. Add the butter, cut it into small pieces, and rub together until the mixture resembles coarse crumbs. Stir in the sugar, mixed peel, and almonds. Work the dough together with your hands, pressing to form a ball. Knead lightly until smooth. Cut the dough in half.

On a lightly floured surface, roll and pat each piece of the dough to a circle 6 inches (15 cm) in diameter. Place on an ungreased cookie sheet. Flute the edges, and with a sharp knife, score each shortbread circle into 8 triangles. Lightly prick all over with a fork.

Bake 30-35 minutes, until very pale in colour. Cut through the markings while the shortbread is still warm. Let cool slightly on the cookie sheet, then cool completely on a wire rack. Sprinkle lightly with sugar.

SCOTTISH FRUIT GRIDDLE SCONES

Classic Scottish scones get their wonderfully light texture and special flavour from being cooked on a griddle or heavy-based skillet on top of the stove. Serve the scones fresh, warm, and oozing with butter and jam. Makes 12.

2 cups	all-purpose flour	500 mL
4 tsp.	baking powder	20 mL
1/2 tsp.	cream of tartar	2 mL
1/4 tsp.	salt	1 mL
1/3 cup	margarine	75 mL
3 tbsp.	sugar	45 mL
1/2 cup	raisins	125 mL
2/3 cup	buttermilk	150 mL

Lightly grease a griddle or heavy-based skillet.

In a mixing bowl, place the flour, baking powder, cream of tartar, and salt. Add the margarine, cut into small pieces, and rub together until the mixture resembles fine crumbs. Stir in the sugar and raisins.

Stir the buttermilk into the flour mixture, mixing just until it forms a ball. Knead very gently on a lightly floured surface, no more than 12 times. Do not overhandle. Cut the dough in half and shape each into a round. Roll each half to a 6 inch (15 cm) circle. Cut each circle into 6 wedges with a sharp knife.

Place the griddle over very low heat until hot. Place the scones 6 at a time on the griddle and cook about 12 minutes, until golden brown underneath. Turn and cook 8-10 minutes longer, until brown on the other side. Remove from the griddle and keep warm, wrapped in a clean tea towel. Cook the remaining 6 scones the same way. Serve warm, split with butter and jam.

DUNDEE CAKE

Dense with plump raisins, glistening cherries, whole almonds, and a blend of fragrant spices, this special fruit cake is perfect for slicing at a Scottish tea.

1 cup	margarine, at room temperature	250 mL
2 1/3 cups	all-purpose flour	575 mL
1/2 tsp.	baking powder	2 mL
1 cup	sugar	250 mL
5	eggs	5
2 cups	currants	500 mL
3 cups	dark raisins	750 mL
1/3 cup	chopped glacé cherries	75 mL
1/2 cup	chopped mixed cut citrus peel	125 mL
1 tsp.	*each* grated orange and lemon rind	5 mL
1 tsp.	ground cinnamon	5 mL
1/2 tsp.	ground ginger	2 mL
1/4 tsp.	*each* ground cloves and nutmeg	1 mL
1/2 cup	whole blanched almonds	125 mL

Heat the oven to 325°F (160°C). Grease and line the bottom and sides of a deep 8 inch (20 cm) round cake tin (a Christmas cake tin is perfect) with waxed paper.

In a large mixing bowl, place the margarine and beat until soft. Add all the remaining ingredients, except the whole almonds, and beat well with a wooden spoon until well mixed, about 3 minutes.

Spoon the mixture into the prepared tin and smooth the top with the back of a wet metal spoon. Arrange the almonds in circles over the top. Bake for about 2 1/4-2 3/4 hours, or until the cake is golden brown and a cake tester inserted in the centre comes out clean. Let cool in the tin for 15 minutes, then turn out, remove the paper, and cool completely on a wire rack. Wrap in foil to store and it will keep for several weeks.

DINNERS

Everyone loves sharing a gorgeous, tasty dinner with special friends or family. In this section are some inspiring ideas for that big occasion: a splendid Mexican Fiesta, a medley of unusual flavours in the Candlelight Feast—and Traditional Christmas Dinner, because you just can't improve on some fine old traditions!

HARVEST CELEBRATION DINNER

Here you will find the perfect blend of harvest flavours—turkey, cranberries, pumpkin, pecans, winter greens—and up-to-date styles of eating and cooking. Get out the heirloom plates and heavy cutlery, and enjoy! Serves 8.

Harvest Pumpkin Bisque
Winter Greens Stuffing
Homemade Country-Style
  Cranberry Sauce
Winter Squash Pie with Whipped
  Cream and Sugared Pecans

Old-fashioned roast turkey
Fresh brussels sprouts with
  lemon butter
Glazed baby carrots

HARVEST PUMPKIN BISQUE

Serve this hot pumpkin bisque in a tureen, or in a warmed pumpkin shell.

4 cups	peeled fresh pumpkin, cut into 1 inch (2.5 cm) cubes	1 L
6 cups	chicken stock	1.5 L
4 tbsp.	butter	60 mL
1	large onion, finely minced	1
2	cloves garlic, minced	2
1 1/2 tsp.	salt	7 mL
1 tsp.	*each* dried thyme and ground ginger	5 mL
4 tbsp.	brown sugar, packed	60 mL
2 tbsp.	fresh lemon juice	30 mL
	freshly ground black pepper to taste	
1 cup	whipping cream	250 mL
	Nutmeg-Thyme Croutons (recipe follows)	

Simmer the pumpkin in the chicken stock until soft and tender, about 25 minutes. Mash the pumpkin to a coarse purée, or transfer to a food processor with a slotted spoon and process. Return the pumpkin to the simmering stock.

In a skillet, heat the butter to bubbling over medium-high heat. Add the minced onion and sauté, stirring, until translucent and pale golden. Stir in the garlic and sauté 1 minute longer. Add the salt, thyme, ginger, and brown sugar. Add this mixture to the simmering stock. Whisk in the lemon juice and liberal grindings black pepper to taste, and heat through 25 minutes, uncovered, over medium heat. Stir the cream into the soup and heat 10 minutes longer. Taste and correct for seasonings. Serve piping hot in warmed bowls. Top each serving with 1/4 cup (50 mL) croutons.

NUTMEG-THYME CROUTONS

6 tbsp.	butter	90 mL
2 tbsp.	vegetable oil	30 mL
2 1/2 cups	white bakery-style bread, crusts removed, cut into 1/4 inch (6 mm) cubes (stale bread, or air-dried several hours)	750 mL
1 tbsp.	dried thyme	15 mL
	ground nutmeg to taste	
	seasoning salt to taste	

Heat the butter and oil in a large non-stick skillet over medium-high heat until sizzling. Add the bread cubes, toss quickly to coat, and fry, stirring, until golden brown and crispy on all sides. Remove from the heat, and toss with the thyme and a light sprinkling of nutmeg and seasoning salt. Cool to room temperature. Serve freshly prepared.

WINTER GREENS STUFFING

This savoury stuffing for your favourite holiday roast turkey makes enough for a 20 lb. (10 kg) bird. The secret to its excellent taste and appearance? A few unusual ingredients: spinach, chard, dried currants, snipped apricots, pine nuts, and a hint of bacon, lemon, and herbs. Makes 12 cups (3 L).

12 cups	Italian or French bread, cut into 1/2 inch (1 cm) cubes, crusts removed	3 L
3/4 cup	dried currants	175 mL
1/2 cup	snipped dried apricots	125 mL
2/3 cup	water	150 mL
2 lbs.	*each* fresh Swiss chard and spinach, stemmed and chopped into 1 inch (2.5 cm) pieces	1 kg
1/2 cup	butter	125 mL
2	large leeks, sliced	2
2	large onions, coarsely diced	2
4 oz.	prosciutto, coarsely diced	125 g
1/2 cup	minced fresh parsley	125 mL
2 tsp.	*each* dried thyme and marjoram	10 mL
1 tbsp.	dried sage	15 mL
	grated rind of 1 large lemon	
3 tbsp.	fresh lemon juice	45 mL
1 cup	pine nuts, toasted in a 325°F (160°C) oven 8-10 minutes and cooled	250 mL
4	eggs, beaten	4
3 cups	chicken stock, warmed	750 mL
	salt and freshly ground black pepper to taste	

Air-dry the bread cubes overnight. Cover the currants and apricots in warm water and soak 20 minutes. Drain. Bring the 2/3 cup (150 mL) water to a boil in a very large stock pot. Add the chard, then the spinach. Partially cover and cook the greens 5 minutes, just until wilted. Drain at once, rinse with cold water until cooled, drain again and squeeze completely dry.

Melt the butter in a large pot over medium-high heat. Add the leeks and onion and sauté until softened and pale golden. Add the wilted greens, prosciutto, parsley, thyme, marjoram, sage, lemon rind, and lemon juice. Sauté 2-3 minutes. Remove from the heat and add the bread cubes, currants and apricots, toasted pine nuts, eggs, and just enough of the warm chicken stock to bind the stuffing together. Season to taste with salt and pepper. Cool completely before stuffing the turkey cavity and neck.

HOMEMADE COUNTRY-STYLE CRANBERRY SAUCE

This lovely fresh cranberry sauce can be prepared up to 2 weeks in advance, capped tightly in jars, and chilled. Serve chilled or cool. Makes 4 cups (1 L).

1 cup	*each* water and sugar	250 mL
1/2 cup	freshly squeezed orange juice	125 mL
12 oz.	fresh cranberries, rinsed and drained	360 g
1/2 cup	honey or maple syrup	125 mL
1 tbsp.	finely grated orange rind	15 mL
1/2 cup	diced pecans, toasted in a	125 mL
	325°F (160°C) oven 8-10 minutes and cooled	

Bring the water and sugar to a simmer over medium-high heat and simmer 5 minutes until the sugar is dissolved. Add the orange juice and cranberries and cook, uncovered, until the berries begin to pop open. Stir in the honey and orange rind, and cook 5 minutes longer, until the cranberries have popped and the liquid is syrupy. Remove from the heat and stir in the pecans. Cool completely. Transfer to clean glass jars, cover with squares of waxed paper, and cap tightly. Refrigerate until serving.

WINTER SQUASH PIE WITH WHIPPED CREAM AND SUGARED PECANS

Here is a delicious alternative to pumpkin pie. Fragrant with spices, and utterly delicious, it is equally successful made with any squash: banana, hubbard, acorn, or butternut.

1	9 inch (23 cm) unbaked deep dish pie shell, or 1 14 oz. (400 g) pkg. frozen pie pastry, thawed and rolled to fit a deep 9 inch (23 cm) pie dish	1
1	2 lb. (1 kg) squash, quartered and seeded	1
1 tsp.	salt	5 mL
1 tsp.	*each* ground cinnamon, nutmeg, and ginger	5 mL
1/2 tsp.	ground allspice	2 mL
1 tbsp.	all-purpose flour	15 mL
1/2 cup	molasses	125 mL
5	eggs, at room temperature	5
2 3/4 cups	whipping cream	675 mL
1 tsp.	vanilla	5 mL
	Sugared Pecans (recipe follows)	

Line a pie dish with pastry, prick the bottom and sides, and chill 1 hour while preparing the filling. Steam the squash over boiling water 30 minutes until very soft and tender. Cool, scoop out the flesh, and mash or purée. The cooked squash should measure a generous 2 1/2 cups (625 mL).

Combine the cooked squash with the salt, cinnamon, nutmeg, ginger, allspice, and flour. Whisk in the molasses and stir until thoroughly combined. Beat the eggs until light and whisk in 3/4 cup (175 mL) of the whipping cream until smooth. Combine both mixtures, mixing thoroughly. Heat the oven to 450°F (230°C).

Place the pie shell on a baking sheet. Carefully pour the filling into the pie, taking care not to spill it over the edges. Place in the lower third of the oven and bake 10 minutes. Reduce the heat to 325°F (160°C), and bake 45-55 minutes longer, or until golden brown and set (when the baking sheet is moved, the filling should not jiggle).

Remove the pie from the oven and allow to cool completely 2-3 hours. Beat the remaining 2 cups (500 mL) whipping cream with the vanilla until it forms soft peaks. Serve the pie accompanied by the whipped cream and a spoonful of Sugared Pecans on top.

SUGARED PECANS

3 tbsp.	butter	45 mL
1 1/2 cups	diced pecans	375 mL
1/3 cup	sugar	75 mL
1/2 tsp.	ground cinnamon	2 mL

Melt the butter in a skillet over medium heat until sizzling. Add the diced pecans and sauté, stirring, 8-10 minutes. The pecans should just turn a nice golden brown (take care not to burn them). Place the pecans in a bowl. Combine the sugar and cinnamon, and pour over the nuts. Toss and shake the bowl to coat the pecans. Pour out onto a brown paper bag to cool. Serve within 4-5 hours.

TRADITIONAL CHRISTMAS DINNER

There is no time like Christmas to bring out the traditionalist in all of us. And Christmas dinner is one of the big reasons! This classic menu features all of the favourites. Happy holidays! Serves 12.

Turkey with All the Trimmings   *Cranberry sauce*
Brussels Sprouts with   *Mincemeat tarts*
  Buttered Crumbs
Steamed Pudding with Orange
  Brandy Sauce

TURKEY WITH ALL THE TRIMMINGS

Timing for roasting a turkey has many variables, but you know it is done when the leg moves easily in the socket, the meat has pulled away from the tip of the leg, and, when the turkey is pierced just above the thigh, the juices run clear. Do not wait until there are no juices, as this will mean a dry bird. If you are using an instant thermometer, it should read 170°F (75°C). If the turkey cooks too fast, don't worry—it will wait for you. Cook the bird on its back, with a little foil over the breastbone, removing the foil for the last hour of roasting time.

1	10-24 lb. (5-12 kg) turkey	1
	Old-Fashioned Bread Stuffing (recipe follows)	
	Pan Gravy (recipe follows)	

Heat the oven to 325-350°F (160-180°C). Stuff the turkey and place on a rack in a shallow pan. Cover loosely with foil and roast according to the weight of the turkey: 4-5 hours for 10-14 lbs. (5-7 kg), 5-6 hours for 15-18 lbs. (7.5-9 kg), 6-7 1/2 hours for 19-24 lbs. (9.5-12 kg). For turkeys over 24 lbs. (12 kg) add 15 minutes per lb. (30 minutes per kg). Baste with pan juices every 30 minutes. Remove the foil for the last hour.

If you are roasting the bird unstuffed, deduct 5 minutes per lb. (10 minutes per kg) from the roasting time.

OLD-FASHIONED BREAD STUFFING

Nothing tastes more like Christmas than a sandwich of bread stuffing and cranberries the day after a huge turkey dinner, or hot bread stuffing and gravy for lunch, so make lots! This recipe makes enough to stuff a 14-16 lb. (7-8 kg) bird.

4 cups	diced celery	1 L
2 cups	chopped onion	500 mL
1 cup	butter	250 mL
4 qts.	bread cubes	4 L
1 tbsp.	salt	15 mL
1 1/2 tsp.	poultry seasoning, or to taste	7 mL
1/2 tsp.	sage, or to taste	2 mL
1/2 tsp.	freshly ground black pepper	2 mL
	chicken stock or canned broth	

Cook the celery and onion in the butter in a large skillet over medium heat until the onion is tender, about 15 minutes.

In a large bowl, toss the bread cubes with the seasonings. Spoon the hot celery and onion mixture over the bread and toss well. Add enough broth to moisten.

Cool before stuffing the turkey. Any extra stuffing can be baked alongside the turkey for the last 30 minutes of cooking time. Spoon turkey drippings over the separately baked stuffing for extra flavour.

Always remove the stuffing from the turkey after roasting, and refrigerate it separately.

PAN GRAVY

If you use turkey drippings for gravy, strain and remove some of the excess fat. This recipe doubles and triples well. Makes 2 cups (500 mL).

4 tbsp.	turkey or chicken fat	60 mL
4 tbsp.	all-purpose flour	60 mL
2 cups	pan juices and chicken stock or canned broth	500 mL
2 tbsp.	concentrated chicken bovril	30 mL
	salt and pepper to taste	

In the roasting pan or a medium saucepan, heat the fat and whisk in the flour. Gradually stir in the pan juices. Cook, stirring or whisking constantly, until thickened and smooth. Add the bovril, taste for seasonings, and add salt and pepper to taste.

The Easy Gourmet features a photograph of this recipe on page 89.

BRUSSELS SPROUTS WITH BUTTERED CRUMBS

An elegant miniature cabbage, brussels sprouts are a traditional Christmas vegetable. The bonus? They have a scant 55 calories per serving, and they are full of vitamin A, potassium, and phosphorus.

2 lbs.	brussels sprouts	1 kg
2 cups	coarse bread crumbs	500 mL
4 tbsp.	butter	60 mL

Trim any ragged leaves from the brussels sprouts. Slice a bit off the stem end of each. Place in a large pot and cover with water. Bring to a boil and cook, uncovered, until the bases of the sprouts are just barely tender when pierced with a thin knife. Place in a shallow ovenproof casserole.

Heat the broiler. Toss the bread crumbs in the melted butter and sprinkle over top of the sprouts. Broil until the crumbs are golden.

The Easy Gourmet features a photograph of this recipe on page 89.

STEAMED PUDDING
WITH ORANGE BRANDY SAUCE

Steamed in a pudding bowl or traditional pudding mold, this rich treat may become your family's own holiday tradition the first time you serve it!

1 cup	grated carrot	250 mL
1 cup	grated potato	250 mL
1 cup	grated apple	250 mL
1 cup	raisins	250 mL
1 cup	currants	250 mL
1 cup	brown sugar	250 mL
1 cup	finely chopped suet or butter	250 mL
2 tbsp.	molasses	30 mL
2	eggs	2
1/2 cup	all-purpose flour	125 mL
1/2 tsp.	*each* cloves, nutmeg, cinnamon, and allspice	2 mL
1/2 tsp.	baking soda	2 mL
	Orange Brandy Sauce (recipe follows)	

In a large bowl, mix together the carrot, potato, apple, raisins and currants. In a medium bowl, cream together the brown sugar, suet, molasses, and eggs. Stir into the carrot mixture. In a small bowl, mix together the flour, spices, and baking soda. Stir into the carrot mixture and mix well.

Spoon into a greased mold. Seal well with foil or a lid. Place on a rack in a large pot. Add boiling water until it is two-thirds of the way up the side of the mold. Bring to a boil over high heat. Reduce the heat to a low simmer, cover, and steam 5-6 hours. Remove from the water bath and cool. Remove from the mold and wrap well. The pudding may be frozen at this point.

To reheat, place the mold in a hot water bath and simmer until heated through, about 1 1/2 hours. Or wrap in plastic wrap and heat in the microwave on HIGH 100% power for 15 minutes. Pierce the mold with a metal skewer. It should be hot to the touch. Serve with Orange Brandy Sauce.

ORANGE BRANDY SAUCE

This sauce is simply heavenly served over the warm Steamed Pudding, but you can also spoon it over pancakes or waffles, or pack it in a pretty crock and give it as a gift. Makes 1 cup (250 mL).

1/2 cup	butter	125 mL
1 cup	icing sugar	250 mL
3 tbsp.	brandy	45 mL
1 tsp.	grated orange rind	5 mL
1 tsp.	orange juice	5 mL
1 tsp.	lemon juice	5 mL
pinch	grated nutmeg	pinch

Cream the butter and icing sugar until very light. Add the remaining ingredients and beat well. Pack into a crock and refrigerate. (The sauce improves over time.)

The Easy Gourmet features a photograph of this recipe on page 89.

MEXICAN FIESTA

Mexican cuisine is enjoying a new popularity, and no wonder! In this menu, lively flavours, gorgeous colours, and excellent nutrition team up for a change-of-pace dinner that is perfect for entertaining. Invite some special friends, put on some salsa music, and watch those winter blues disappear. Serves 4.

Prawns with Cilantro Sauce
Quesadillas Stuffed with
  Mushrooms

Warm flour tortillas
Assorted red and green salsas

PRAWNS WITH CILANTRO SAUCE

This dipping dish is designed for a gathering of good friends. It is inspired by the cuisine of Mexico, where the prawns are huge, so choose the largest ones available.

2 qts.	water	2 L
1	small onion, quartered	1
1	clove garlic	1
1	bay leaf	1
1	sprig fresh thyme	1
1	sprig fresh oregano or marjoram	1
4	whole peppercorns	4
40-50	large prawns, in the shell, about 1 1/2 lbs. (750 g)	40-50
	sprigs of fresh cilantro and slices of lime for garnish	
	Cilantro Sauce (recipe follows)	

Put the water in a large pot along with the onion, garlic, bay leaf, thyme, oregano, and peppercorns. Bring to a rolling boil. Add the prawns and cook 3 minutes or until the shells turn pink. Drain and cool the prawns. Discard the cooking water. Chill the prawns in the refrigerator.

To serve, arrange the prawns on a serving platter and garnish with sprigs of cilantro and slices of lime. Serve the sauce on the side and invite guests to peel their prawns and dip in the sauce.

CILANTRO SAUCE

1/2 cup	yogurt or sour cream	125 mL
1/2 cup	whipping cream	125 mL
2 cups	fresh cilantro, loosely packed	500 mL
2	cloves garlic	2
4	green onions, coarsely chopped	4
pinch	freshly ground black pepper	pinch

Blend all ingredients in a blender or food processor until smooth. Transfer to a glass serving bowl and refrigerate until well chilled, about 2 hours.

The Easy Gourmet features a photograph of this recipe on page 107.

QUESADILLAS STUFFED WITH MUSHROOMS

Quesadillas are flour tortillas spread with a thin layer of filling, topped with another tortilla, and lightly refried. Serve with green and red salsas, as spicy as you like them.

2 tbsp.	olive oil	30 mL
2 tbsp.	butter	30 mL
2	cloves garlic, minced	2
4 tbsp.	finely chopped onion	60 mL
1	small jalapeño pepper, finely chopped	1
1 lb.	fresh mushrooms, finely chopped	500 g
3 tbsp.	chopped fresh cilantro	45 mL
	salt and pepper to taste	
8	8 inch (20 cm) flour tortillas	8
4 tbsp.	shredded Monterey jack cheese	60 mL

Heat the oil and butter in a large skillet over medium-low heat and sauté the garlic and onion until tender. Add the jalapeño and mushrooms (never touch your eyes after you've handled the peppers—they're hot!) and cook until the

Opposite: Mexican Fiesta (pp. 105-109)—Prawns with Cilantro Sauce, Quesadillas Stuffed with Mushrooms.

mushrooms have released their juices. Drain off some of the liquid. Add the cilantro and season with salt and pepper. Simmer over low heat 20 minutes or until the mixture thickens. Remove from the heat and set aside.

For each quesadilla, spread the mushroom mixture thinly over a flour tortilla, sprinkle on 1 tbsp. (15 mL) of the cheese, top with another tortilla, and press together. Heat a medium skillet and brush with a little olive oil. Sauté the quesadillas, one at a time, until the tortillas are lightly browned on both sides, about 2 minutes.

To serve, cut into 6-8 triangles. Place the red and green salsas in small lettuce cups and arrange beside the triangles. Serve immediately.

The Easy Gourmet features a photograph of this recipe on page 107.

EW-WAVE ITALIAN DINNER

New versions of old classics are being cooked and enjoyed in Italy. This menu takes full advantage of the taste of Italian cooking that we know and love, and adds some unique contemporary touches. Serves 4.

Asparagus Flan with Maltaise Sauce
Fried Polenta

ASPARAGUS FLAN WITH MALTAISE SAUCE

Here is your chance to discover Maltaise Sauce, a thickened hollandaise with orange flavouring. Store it in a vacuum jug until serving time and serve with your own warm pasta salad and Fried Polenta (recipe follows).

3 lbs.	fresh asparagus, cooked, puréed, and well drained	1.5 kg
	(about 1 1/2 cups (375 mL) puréed vegetable)	
1 cup	whipping cream	250 mL
6	egg yolks	6
	freshly ground black pepper and nutmeg to taste	
8	asparagus tips, cooked, for garnish	8
	Maltaise Sauce (recipe follows)	

Heat the oven to 375°F (190°C). Mix together the puréed asparagus, cream, and egg yolks. Season to taste with pepper and nutmeg. Pour into a well-greased 9 inch (23 cm) quiche dish or individual ramekins. Place in a large pan of hot water and bake 20 minutes or until a knife inserted slightly off centre comes out clean. Garnish with the asparagus tips. Serve with Maltaise Sauce spooned over top.

MALTAISE SAUCE

1/2 cup	butter	125 mL
3	egg yolks, at room temperature	3
	salt and pepper to taste	
2 tbsp.	finely grated orange rind	30 mL

Melt the butter to boiling in a small saucepan. Place the egg yolks and seasonings in a blender. With the machine running, very slowly pour in the hot butter until the mixture becomes a thin mayonnaise. Season to taste with salt and pepper and add the orange rind. Store in a vacuum jug until serving time. Reheat gently over very low heat.

FRIED POLENTA

Cut this delicious corn meal dough into fun shapes and fry it up for a tasty snack or a nutritious addition to an Italian dinner. Makes 20 rounds, each 2 1/2 inches (6 cm).

6 tbsp.	butter	90 mL
1	medium onion, chopped	1
3 1/2 cups	water	875 mL
1 cup	yellow corn meal	250 mL
pinch	salt	pinch
2 tbsp.	chopped fresh parsley	30 mL
4 tbsp.	grated Parmesan cheese	60 mL
	chopped tomato and green onion for garnish	

In a microproof bowl, melt 4 tbsp. (60 mL) of the butter on HIGH 100% power. Add the onion and cook about 1 minute on HIGH 100% power. Add the water and heat on HIGH 100% power about 5 minutes until the water is hot. Stir in the corn meal and salt and cook 5 minutes longer on HIGH 100% power, stirring every 2 minutes. It should be thick and creamy. Stir in the parsley and cheese. Pour onto a greased flat surface to a thickness of 3/4-1 inch (2-2.5 cm) and cool thoroughly.

Cut into shapes and dust with flour. Heat the remaining 2 tbsp. (30 mL) butter in a skillet and fry the polenta until crisp and golden on both sides. Garnish with chopped tomato and green onion, and serve immediately.

The Easy Gourmet features a photograph of this recipe on the front cover.

CELEBRATION DINNER FOR TWO

Sometimes the most important people you can entertain are you and that special person. Next time you want to celebrate each other, try this exclusive, elegant dinner. Dress the table with your prettiest linen, add flowers, candles, and your best china and glassware, and the stage is set for a perfect memory. Serves 2.

Carrot and Orange Soup
Cornish Game Hens with
  Fruit Stuffing
Broccoli Timbales with Red
  Pepper Sauce
Chocolate Crême Brulée

Crisp green salad
Potato croquettes

CARROT AND ORANGE SOUP

Smooth and velvety, this is just the soup to start off that special dinner! It freezes well, so it can be made ahead and heated through at serving time.

2 tbsp.	butter	30 mL
1 cup	chopped onion	250 mL
1 lb.	carrots, peeled and sliced	500 g
2 cups	chicken stock	500 mL
1/2 cup	orange juice	125 mL
	salt and black pepper to taste	
1/4 tsp.	ground nutmeg	1 mL
4 tbsp.	whipping cream or plain yogurt	60 mL
	grated orange rind for garnish	

Place the butter, onion, and carrots in a microproof casserole dish. Cover and microwave on HIGH 100% power 6-8 minutes until the vegetables are soft, stirring once or twice during the cooking time.

Stir in the chicken stock and orange juice. Purée until smooth.

Return the puréed soup to the casserole dish, season to taste with salt and pepper, and blend in the nutmeg. Cover and microwave on HIGH 100% power until the soup comes to a boil, stirring during the cooking time.

To serve, top each portion with a swirl of whipping cream or yogurt, and sprinkle on grated orange rind to taste.

CORNISH GAME HENS WITH FRUIT STUFFING

Here is a real special-occasion recipe: tender game hens with an unusual combination of fruit flavours and a tasty apricot glaze. Have the Cornish hens boned, then stuff them ahead of time and refrigerate.

2	Cornish game hens, about 1 lb. (500 g) each	2
4 tbsp.	finely chopped prunes	60 mL
4 tbsp.	finely chopped dried apricots	60 mL
1	apple, peeled, cored, and chopped	1
	grated rind of 1 lemon	
2 tbsp.	lemon juice	30 mL
1 cup	fresh bread crumbs	250 mL
1/2 cup	orange juice	125 mL
1/2 cup	apricot jam	125 mL
1 tbsp.	soy sauce	15 mL

Wash the game hens and pat dry with a paper towel.

Mix together the prunes, apricots, apple, lemon rind, 1 tbsp. (15 mL) of the lemon juice, and the bread crumbs. Add orange juice until the mixture reaches a moist consistency.

Pour any extra orange juice into the cavities of the hens. Pack half the stuffing into each hen. Tie the wings and drumsticks in place with fine string or bamboo skewers.

Place the apricot jam, the remaining 1 tbsp. (15 mL) lemon juice and the soy sauce in a small microproof bowl. Microwave on MEDIUM 50% power 1-2 minutes until dissolved. Place the hens in a microproof dish, breast side up. Brush generously with apricot glaze. Microwave on HIGH 100% power, allowing 6-8 minutes per pound (500 g). Halfway through the cooking time, brush with the remaining glaze. Let stand, loosely covered with foil, for about 8 minutes. The hen is done when the leg moves freely and the juices run clear when the inner thigh is pierced with a fork.

At serving time, remove the string or bamboo skewers.

BROCCOLI TIMBALES
WITH RED PEPPER SAUCE

The microwave is the perfect medium for making timbales—the vegetables keep their lovely bright colours and the timbales stay light and moist.

Ramekin

1 cup	coarsely chopped broccoli	250 mL
1/2	small onion, chopped	1/2
1	egg	1
1 tbsp.	whipping cream	15 mL
1/2 tsp.	lemon juice	2 mL
	salt and pepper to taste	

Sauce

1	large red bell pepper, seeded and chopped	1
1 tbsp.	butter	15 mL
4 tbsp.	whipping cream	60 mL

Butter two individual ramekin dishes. Set aside.

Place the broccoli and onion in a microproof dish. Cover and microwave on HIGH 100% power 5-8 minutes until the vegetables are soft, stirring halfway through the cooking time.

Reserve 2 pieces of broccoli for garnish. Add the remaining broccoli and onion to a blender, together with the egg, cream and lemon juice. Purée until smooth. Season with salt and pepper. Divide between the prepared ramekin dishes. (You may cover the dishes with plastic wrap and refrigerate at this point.) To cook, microwave the covered dishes on MEDIUM 50% power 4-6 minutes until the centres are barely set. Let stand, covered, for 2-3 minutes.

To make the sauce, place the red pepper and butter in a microproof dish. Cover and microwave on HIGH 100% power 4-6 minutes until the pepper is soft. Let cool slightly and purée with the cream. (The sauce can be refrigerated at this point.) To heat, microwave on MEDIUM 50% power until heated through.

To serve, place the sauce on serving plates and unmold the ramekins onto the sauce. Garnish each serving with a piece of reserved broccoli.

CHOCOLATE CRÈME BRULÉE

"To die and go to heaven" is how this dessert has been described! There can be no better ending for a Celebration Dinner for Two. This recipe makes four portions, because you'll want extras to chill and serve later.

3	egg yolks	3
2 tsp.	sugar	10 mL
1 tsp.	cornstarch	5 mL
1 cup	whipping cream	250 mL
3 oz.	semi-sweet chocolate, grated	90 g
1/2 cup	sifted icing sugar	125 mL
	strawberries or raspberries for garnish	

In a small dish, cream together the egg yolks, sugar, and cornstarch.

Place the cream in a 4 cup (1 L) microproof measure. Microwave on HIGH 100% power 1-2 minutes to bring to a boil. Blend a bit of the cream into the egg yolk mixture. Mix well and return to the remaining cream in the measure. Stir well.

Microwave on MEDIUM 50% power in 1 minute increments until the mixture is thickened, stirring well after each cooking period.

Place the chocolate in a small microproof dish. Microwave on MEDIUM 50% power until melted. Blend into the custard mixture and divide equally among four individual 1/2 cup (125 mL) ramekin dishes. Refrigerate until chilled.

To serve, sift a thick cushion of icing sugar onto each portion. Place under a hot broiler until the sugar is caramelized. Serve immediately, garnished with berries.

SPICY CURRY DINNER

An exotic menu inspired by the cuisine of India, this collection of recipes can be mastered by even the beginning cook. Take advantage of some convenience foods, then prepare this delicious, pungently fragrant array of dishes, and don't plan on leftovers! Serves 4.

Chicken Vindaloo
Vegetable Briyani
Sweet Lassi

Tomato and cucumber salad
Assorted chutneys

CHICKEN VINDALOO

This is a wonderfully spicy, rather than hot, version of a classic eastern dish. It is even better made a day before serving, so all the flavours can blend.

4 tbsp.	butter or margarine	60 mL
2	medium onions, chopped	2
3	cloves garlic, crushed	3
2 tsp.	finely chopped fresh ginger	10 mL
1 tsp.	mustard seeds	5 mL
1	3 lb. (1.5 kg) frying chicken, cut in small joints and skinned	1
1 tbsp.	curry powder	15 mL
1 tsp.	*each* turmeric, coriander, and paprika	5 mL
1/2 tsp.	chili powder	2 mL
1/4 tsp.	salt	1 mL
1/2 cup	water	125 mL
2	medium tomatoes, cored and coarsely chopped	2
4 tbsp.	tomato paste	60 mL
2	bay leaves	2
1	2 inch (5 cm) piece cinnamon stick	1
8	whole cloves	8
1 lb.	potatoes, peeled and cut in 1 1/2 inch (4 cm) chunks	500 g
1 tbsp.	lemon juice or vinegar	15 mL
1/3 cup	fine unsweetened dried coconut	75 mL

In a large saucepan, melt the butter. Add the onion, garlic, ginger, and mustard seeds and sauté over medium heat 8-10 minutes, until the onion is soft and golden brown. Stir in the chicken and cook over medium heat 5 minutes, stirring occasionally. Reduce the heat to low. Stir in the curry, turmeric, coriander, paprika, chili, salt, and water. Cover and cook 5 minutes over low heat.

Stir in the tomatoes, tomato paste, bay leaves, cinnamon stick, and cloves. Simmer 20 minutes, covered. Add the potatoes, lemon juice, and coconut. Stir well and simmer, covered, about 15 minutes or until the potatoes and chicken are cooked. Add a little more water if desired for a thinner gravy. Remove the bay leaves and cinnamon stick and serve.

VEGETABLE BRIYANI

In this dish, rice takes on a special touch of glamour. Fragrant Indian basmati rice is mixed with colourful vegetables and spices, and a dash of turmeric gives it a lovely golden hue.

4 tbsp.	butter or margarine	60 mL
1	medium onion, chopped	1
2	cloves garlic, crushed	2
1 tsp.	finely chopped fresh ginger	5 mL
1 tsp.	mustard seeds	5 mL
1 1/2 cups	basmati rice	375 mL
1/2 tsp.	salt	2 mL
1 cup	sliced carrots	250 mL
1 cup	frozen peas	250 mL
2	bay leaves	2
1	2 inch (5 cm) piece cinnamon stick	1
6	whole cloves	6
1 tsp.	turmeric	5 mL

In a large, heavy-based saucepan, melt the butter. Add the onion, garlic, ginger, and mustard seeds and sauté 8-10 minutes over medium heat, until the onion is soft and pale golden. Add the rice and stir for 1 minute. Add 2 cups (500 mL) cold water. Stir in the salt and carrots. Bring to a boil, then reduce the heat and cook over low heat, covered, for 5 minutes.

Add the peas, bay leaves, cinnamon, cloves, and turmeric. Cook over low heat, covered, for 10 minutes. When the water has been absorbed, stir lightly. Cover and cook over very low heat 5 minutes longer to steam-cook the rice. Remove the bay leaves and cinnamon stick, and serve.

SWEET LASSI

This sweet yogurt drink is traditional with curry dishes, as it perfectly complements the spiciness. Serve it cold and frothy with lots of ice.

2 cups	plain yogurt	500 mL
1/2 cup	cold water	125 mL
4 tbsp.	sugar	60 mL
	ice cubes	

In a large mixing bowl, beat the yogurt with a wire whisk until smooth. Whisk in the water, then the sugar, beating until frothy. (For a thinner drink, add a little more water.) Pour into tall glasses and serve immediately with lots of ice cubes.

Note: A more tart lassi can be made by omitting the sugar and adding 1/2 tsp. (2 mL) salt and a few grindings of black pepper.

CANDLELIGHT FEAST

This menu is full of the special flavours and colours of the winter holiday season, but it is unusual enough to start new traditions. Most of these unique dishes can be prepared ahead, leaving you free to be with your guests—and then amaze them with your culinary skills! Serves 8.

Mango and Avocado Salad
Stuffed Holiday Ham
Parmesan Vegetable Medley
Chestnut and Orange Soufflé with Raspberry Sauce
Curried Roast Potatoes

MANGO AND AVOCADO SALAD

Give your special dinner a sparkling fresh start with this fruity appetizer. The mayonnaise dressing can be made ahead and refrigerated for 2-3 days.

3 tbsp.	olive oil	45 mL
4 tbsp.	lemon juice	60 mL
1	large clove garlic, crushed	1
1/4 tsp.	*each* salt and pepper	1 mL
pinch	cayenne pepper	pinch
2/3 cup	mayonnaise	150 mL
1/3 cup	whipping cream	75 mL
1/3 cup	chopped fresh flowering chives	75 mL
3	ripe mangos	3
4	ripe avocados	4
6	slices bacon, finely chopped and fried until crisp	6

In a small bowl, combine the olive oil, lemon juice, garlic, salt, pepper, and cayenne. Beat in the mayonnaise and cream, then the chives. Set aside. (Refrigerate at this point if you are making it ahead.)

When ready to serve, peel and slice the mangos and arrange them on salad plates. Halve the avocados, remove the pits, and peel. Slice thinly. Arrange one avocado half on each salad plate in a fan shape. Spoon the dressing over the avocado and sprinkle the bacon over the mango.

STUFFED HOLIDAY HAM

When you cut this ham at serving time, it falls into pretty slices that show off the tasty green stuffing and the delicate pink of the meat—a perfect holiday colour and flavour combination.

1	5 lb. (2.5 kg) smoked boneless ham	1
1 tsp.	Worcestershire sauce	5 mL
1/4 tsp.	ground cloves	1 mL
2 1/2 tbsp.	butter or margarine	37 mL
3/4 cup	finely chopped onion	175 mL
2	cloves garlic, crushed	2
1	11 oz. (300 g) pkg. frozen chopped spinach, cooked and drained	1
1 tbsp.	all-purpose flour	15 mL
1/3 cup	chicken broth	75 mL
1 1/2 tbsp.	Dijon mustard	22 mL
1 tbsp.	whipping cream	15 mL
pinch	curry powder	pinch
	salt and pepper to taste	
1/2 cup	grated emmenthal cheese	125 mL
3 tbsp.	grated Romano cheese	45 mL

Place the ham in a roasting pan and cut 1/2 inch (1 cm) thick slices, three-quarters of the way through the ham. Rub the Worcestershire sauce and cloves all over the ham. Set aside.

In a medium saucepan, melt 2 tbsp. (30 mL) of the butter and sauté the onion and garlic over medium heat until soft but not brown. Stir in the spinach and cook, stirring, for 1-2 minutes until all the liquid has evaporated. Remove from the heat and purée in a food processor or blender. Allow to cool.

Heat the oven to 350°F (180°C). In a small saucepan, melt the remaining 1/2 tbsp. (7 mL) butter. Add the flour and cook, stirring, for 30 seconds. Remove from the heat and gradually stir in the broth. Return to the heat and cook, stirring constantly, until the mixture thickens and boils. Stir in the mustard, cream, curry powder, salt, and pepper. Cook for about 4 minutes, stirring over medium heat until well thickened.

Fill the slits in the ham with the spinach mixture and spread it over the ham, too. Spread mustard sauce over the top. Sprinkle the cheeses over the sauce and press in. (The dish can be prepared ahead to this point and refrigerated.) Bake 1 hour until golden brown. Allow to cool slightly before slicing.

PARMESAN VEGETABLE MEDLEY

Packed with the colours of the season, this unusual combination of vegetables is both wholesome and festive.

4 oz.	fresh or frozen snow peas, trimmed	125 g
4 cups	broccoli florets	1000 mL
1/2 lb.	green beans, trimmed	250 g
1 lb.	cherry tomatoes	500 g
4 tbsp.	olive oil	60 mL
4 tbsp.	melted butter	60 mL
2 tbsp.	chopped fresh parsley	30 mL
1/2 tsp.	dried basil	2 mL
2	cloves garlic, crushed	2
4 tbsp.	grated Parmesan cheese	60 mL
1/3 cup	pine nuts or slivered almonds	75 mL

Heat the oven to 350°F (180°C).

Place the snow peas, broccoli, and green beans in a vegetable steamer set over a pan of simmering water. Steam 4 minutes. Place in a casserole dish with the cherry tomatoes, tossing together to mix.

In a small bowl, combine the olive oil, butter, parsley, basil, and garlic. Pour over the vegetables and sprinkle with the Parmesan and pine nuts. (The dish can be prepared ahead to this point and refrigerated.)

Bake 15-20 minutes, until the dish is heated through and the tomatoes are cooked.

CHESTNUT AND ORANGE SOUFFLÉ WITH RASPBERRY SAUCE

Lusciously smooth and fragrant with the flavours of chestnut and orange, this impressive company dish can be made ahead and decorated at the last minute.

6	medium eggs	6
2/3 cup	sugar	150 mL
2	envelopes unflavoured gelatin	2
2/3 cup	cold water	150 mL
1/3 cup	fresh orange juice	75 mL
2	8 3/4 oz. (250 g) cans sweetened chestnut purée	2
1 1/2 tsp.	grated orange rind	7 mL
1 1/3 cups	whipping cream	325 mL

Raspberry Sauce

2	15 oz. (425 g) pkgs. frozen raspberries, thawed and drained	2
4 tbsp.	red currant jelly, melted	60 mL
2 tbsp.	icing sugar	30 mL

	toasted chopped nuts, whipped cream, and orange rind for decoration

Wrap a double strip of foil around a 6 cup (1.5 L) soufflé dish, so it extends at least 3 inches (7.5 cm) above the top of the dish. Fasten securely.

Separate the eggs and, in a large bowl set over a pan of simmering water, whisk the egg yolks and 1/3 cup (75 mL) of the sugar with an electric mixer until the mixture is thick and pale and leaves a trail when lifted, about 5 minutes. Remove from the heat. In a small bowl, stir the gelatin into the cold water. Set over a pan of simmering water and stir until dissolved. Remove from the heat and stir in the orange juice. Beat gradually in a thin stream into the egg yolk mixture. Beat in the chestnut purée and the orange rind.

Set the bowl over a larger bowl of ice water and let stand, stirring occasionally, until slightly thickened. This should only take a few minutes. Be careful it doesn't thicken too much.

Meanwhile, beat the egg whites until frothy, then beat in the remaining 1/3 cup (75 mL) sugar until stiff. Beat the whipping cream until stiff. Fold the egg whites into the egg yolk mixture, then fold in the cream. Pour into the soufflé dish and chill several hours.

To make the raspberry sauce, press the raspberries through a fine sieve, then beat in the currant jelly and icing sugar until well mixed. Store in the refrigerator.

To serve, remove the foil from the soufflé dish and press the chopped nuts carefully around the sides. Pipe swirls of whipped cream around the top edge. Decorate with orange rind. Serve with the raspberry sauce.

CURRIED ROAST POTATOES

A touch of curry and the exotic crunch of mustard seeds make these roast potatoes a unique taste treat—your guests will come back for second helpings every time.

4 lbs.	red-skinned potatoes	2 kg
	salt to taste	
1/2 cup	butter or margarine	125 mL
2 tsp.	mustard seeds	10 mL
1 tbsp.	curry powder	15 mL
1 cup	diagonally sliced green onion	250 mL

Heat the oven to 350°F (180°C).

Leaving the skins on, cut the potatoes into 1 1/2-2 inch (3.5-5 cm) chunks. Place in a vegetable steamer set over a pan of simmering water. Steam 10 minutes. Place in a roasting pan or on a large cookie sheet, sprinkle with a little salt, and set aside.

In a small skillet, melt the butter. Add the mustard seeds and curry powder and sauté for 1 minute. Pour this mixture over the potatoes. (The dish can be prepared ahead to this point.)

Bake about 1 hour, turning occasionally, until golden brown. Stir in the green onions for the last 10 minutes of cooking time.

Opposite: Midnight Fondue (pp. 134-35)—(top to bottom) Canadian Cheddar Fondue, Swiss Chocolate Fondue.

ODERN CANTONESE FEAST

The best of Oriental cooking is presented in this dinner: easy preparation, fresh ingredients, exotic flavours, and a cornucopia of colours. Serve it on delicate plates with a set of chopsticks for each guest—east meets west for a special occasion with friends. Serves 6.

Mandarin Garlic Ribs   Boiled rice
Gingered Beef with Peppers   Fresh lychees and wedges of
Chinese Vegetable Stir-Fry   fresh orange

MANDARIN GARLIC RIBS

A big platter of hot, sticky, garlicky ribs, steeped in Oriental spices and served up with a delicious plum sauce for dipping—what more could anyone ask?

2 tbsp.	vegetable oil	30 mL
3 lbs.	pork loin back ribs, cut in 2 inch (5 cm) pieces	1.5 kg
1/3 cup	sugar	75 mL
1 cup	hot water	250 mL
1/3 cup	soy sauce	75 mL
3	large cloves garlic, crushed	3
1/4 tsp.	*each* dried thyme and oregano	1 mL
Plum Sauce		
1/3 cup	honey	75 mL
1/3 cup	dark Chinese plum sauce	75 mL
1 tbsp.	soy sauce	15 mL
1 tbsp.	*each* Chinese cooking wine and molasses	15 mL
2 tbsp.	lemon juice	30 mL
1 tsp.	Worcestershire sauce	5 mL
1	large clove garlic, crushed	1
1/2 tsp.	dry mustard	2 mL

1 tbsp.	cornstarch	15 mL
2 tsp.	cold water	10 mL
	toasted sesame seeds for garnish	

In a large, heavy-based skillet or wok, heat the oil. Fry the ribs over medium heat, stirring often, until golden brown, about 15 minutes. Remove with a slotted spoon and set aside.

Clean the skillet and heat the sugar over medium-low heat, stirring occasionally, until dissolved and golden brown. This will take about 8 minutes. Watch it carefully so it does not burn. Remove from the heat and slowly stir in the hot water. (Be careful, as it may spatter.) Stir over low heat to dissolve the caramelized sugar. Stir in the soy sauce, garlic, thyme, and oregano. Return the ribs to the skillet and cook over low heat, covered, for about 45 minutes, or until tender.

Meanwhile, to make the plum sauce, combine the honey, plum sauce, soy sauce, cooking wine, molasses, lemon juice, Worcestershire sauce, garlic, and mustard. Set aside.

When the ribs are tender, blend together the cornstarch and cold water. Pour into the ribs and cook, stirring, until the sauce is thickened and smooth. Place in a warm serving dish, sprinkle with sesame seeds, and serve with the plum sauce.

GINGERED BEEF WITH PEPPERS

The aromatic flavour of ginger envelops this dish, a quick stir-fry of tender beef, bell peppers, and green onions.

1 lb.	beef round steak, trimmed	500 g
1 tbsp.	cornstarch	15 mL
3 tbsp.	soy sauce	45 mL
3 tbsp.	vegetable oil	45 mL
1/2 tsp.	black pepper	2 mL
3 tbsp.	Chinese cooking wine	45 mL
1 tsp.	sugar	5 mL
2 tbsp.	coarsely grated fresh ginger	30 mL
1	medium onion, cut in coarse wedges	1
1	medium green bell pepper, cored, seeded and diced	1
1 cup	diagonally sliced green onion	250 mL
3 tbsp.	chopped fresh Chinese parsley	45 mL

Cut the beef into thin strips, across the grain. In a mixing bowl, place the cornstarch. Blend in the soy sauce, 1 tbsp. (15 mL) of the vegetable oil and the black pepper. Stir in the beef and marinate for 30 minutes in the refrigerator. In a small bowl, combine the cooking wine and sugar and set aside.

When the beef has marinated, heat the remaining 2 tbsp. (30 mL) oil in a large skillet or wok. Stir in the beef and ginger and sauté over medium-high heat, stirring to break up the pieces, for about 4 minutes, until the meat loses its pink colour. Remove with a slotted spoon and set aside.

Add the onion and pepper to the skillet and cook, stirring, 4-5 minutes over high heat. Return the beef to the skillet. Stir in the wine and sugar mixture, green onion, and Chinese parsley and stir for 30-60 seconds. Serve at once, sprinkled with extra parsley if desired.

CHINESE VEGETABLE STIR-FRY

Have the vegetables prepared ahead, and this dish can be put together in minutes. Many combinations of vegetables besides the ones suggested here work beautifully—select your favourites.

3 tbsp.	vegetable oil	45 mL
1	medium onion, coarsely chopped	1
2	cloves garlic, crushed	2
2 cups	sliced mushrooms	500 mL
1	medium red bell pepper, cored, seeded and sliced	1
4 oz.	snow peas, trimmed	125 g
2 cups	broccoli florets	500 mL
1	8 oz. (227 mL) can sliced water chestnuts, drained	1
1/2 cup	chicken broth or stock	125 mL
1 tbsp.	cornstarch	15 mL
3 tbsp.	soy sauce	45 mL
1 tbsp.	water	15 mL
2 cups	fresh bean sprouts	500 mL
1 cup	roasted cashews	250 mL

In a large skillet or wok, heat the oil. Sauté the onion and garlic over medium-high heat for about 4 minutes. Add the mushrooms, red pepper, snow peas, broccoli, and water chestnuts. Sauté, stirring, for 1 minute. Pour in the chicken broth and simmer 5 minutes.

In a small bowl, combine the cornstarch, soy sauce, and water. Pour into the vegetable mixture and bring to a boil, stirring, until thickened and smooth. Stir in the bean sprouts and cashews and heat through. Place in a heated serving dish and serve.

LATE EVENING

This section offers irresistible complements to after-hours company and conversation, from the mouth-watering Midnight Special to the decadent Dessert Lovers' Smorgasbord.

IRESIDE SNACK

This lovely mid-winter menu is a great focus for a special family get-together. Designed for children and adults alike, the menu looks as good as it tastes—get out your favourite wooden bowls for the apples and nuts, and serve the cheese on a big wooden board. Serves 12.

Hot Spiced Strawberry Punch   *Whipped cream cheese*
Spicy Pumpkin-Nut Bread   *Crisp red and green apples*
Brown Sugar Shortbread   *Assorted nuts in the shell*
   Cut-outs   *Assorted cheeses*

HOT SPICED STRAWBERRY PUNCH

Serve this pretty, spicy strawberry punch in glass mugs, each with a long cinnamon-stick stirrer, or a wooden skewer laced with fresh strawberries.

4 cups	strawberry cocktail	1 L
2 cups	cold water	500 mL
1/3 cup	sugar	75 mL
1/2 cup	fresh lemon juice	125 mL
4	2 inch (5 cm) whole cinnamon sticks	4
24	whole cloves	24
1	small orange	1
1 cup	freshly squeezed orange juice	250 mL
	cinnamon sticks, orange slices or wedges, and	
	wooden skewers threaded with halved fresh strawberries, for garnish	

In a large saucepan, combine the strawberry cocktail, cold water, and sugar. Bring to a simmer, stirring, until the sugar is dissolved. Add the lemon juice and cinnamon sticks. Stick the cloves into the whole orange and add to the simmering mixture. Simmer 15 minutes. Add the orange juice. Simmer 5 minutes. Ladle the hot punch into glass mugs and garnish as suggested.

SPICY PUMPKIN-NUT BREAD

You can bake this wonderful spiced pumpkin bread up to 3 days ahead of time, as it keeps very well. Wrap tightly until serving time. Serve in slices, accompanied by a bowl of whipped cream cheese for spreading.

3 1/2 cups	all-purpose flour	875 mL
2 tsp.	baking soda	10 mL
3/4 tsp.	baking powder	3 mL
1 1/2 tsp.	salt	7 mL
1 tsp.	*each* ground cinnamon and nutmeg	5 mL
1/2 tsp.	*each* ground cloves, ginger, and allspice	2 mL
2 cups	cooked, mashed pumpkin (canned pumpkin is ideal)	500 mL
2/3 cup	*each* vegetable oil and cold water	150 mL
2 2/3 cup	sugar	650 mL
2	eggs, at room temperature	2
2 tbsp.	finely grated orange rind	30 mL
1 cup	diced walnuts or pecans	250 mL
1/2 cup	raisins (optional)	125 mL

Heat the oven to 350°F (180°C). Grease two 8 x 5 x 3 inch (20 x 12.5 x 7.5 cm) loaf pans and dust lightly with flour. Set aside. Sift together the flour, baking soda, baking powder, salt, cinnamon, nutmeg, cloves, ginger, and allspice. Set aside.

Beat together the pumpkin, vegetable oil, cold water, sugar, eggs, and orange rind 3 minutes or until very smooth. Add the flour mixture, a third at a time, beating well after each addition until the batter is smooth. Gently stir in the nuts and raisins. Divide the batter and pour into the prepared pans. Bake in the centre of the heated oven 60-75 minutes. The tops will be characteristically "cracked" down the middle, a wooden skewer inserted in the centre will come out clean, and the loaves will spring back when gently pressed.

Cool the loaves 10 minutes in their pans on wire racks, then turn out onto the racks and cool completely before serving, 2-3 hours.

BROWN SUGAR SHORTBREAD CUT-OUTS

This delicately brown shortbread with its slightly nutty flavour is the best reason to bring out your favourite holiday cookie cutters—reindeers, stars, angels, trees, bells, the works. Makes about 3-4 dozen cookies. If you double the recipe, prepare each batch of dough separately.

1 cup	softened butter	250 mL
1 1/4 cups	dark brown sugar, firmly packed	300 mL
1 tsp.	vanilla	5 mL
pinch	salt	pinch
2 cups	sifted all-purpose flour	500 mL
1/2 cup	very finely ground toasted filberts	125 mL
	(toast the nuts in a shallow pan in a 325°F (160°C)	
	oven 8 minutes, cool completely, and grind to a flour-like consistency)	

Cream the butter until light and fluffy. Add the brown sugar, beating until very creamy and light. Add the vanilla and salt. Whisk together the flour and nuts to combine. Gradually add the dry ingredients to the creamed mixture, beating until smooth. Gather the dough and pat into a slightly flattened ball. Wrap in plastic wrap and chill 1-2 hours to firm.

Heat the oven to 300°F (150°C). Roll out the dough on a lightly floured surface to a thickness of 1/4 inch (6 mm). Cut out with floured cookie cutters. Place the cookies on a lightly greased baking sheet (or line the sheets with baking parchment). Bake about 20 minutes or until golden. Cool on the sheets 5 minutes, then transfer to wire racks to cool completely.

MIDNIGHT FONDUE

Fondue never goes out of fashion. It is delicious and nutritious, a little goes a long way, and it makes a great party! If you have a well-worn oak table, chequered napkins, and rustic dinnerware, now is the time to bring them out. Fresh flowers and hearty loaves of bread make a lovely centrepiece. Serves 6.

Canadian Cheddar Fondue
Swiss Chocolate Fondue

Mixed green salad with
vinaigrette dressing
Thin slices of smoked turkey
and Black Forest ham

CANADIAN CHEDDAR FONDUE

Here is a truly Canadian version of the classic fondue. Sharp and tangy with the flavour of fine aged cheddar, it is wonderful served hot and bubbly with cubes of crusty whole grain bread for dipping.

1	12 oz. (355 mL) bottle ale or amber beer (or dry cider or non-alcoholic beer)	1
1 lb.	sharp Canadian cheddar cheese, coarsely grated	500 g
1 tbsp.	cornstarch	15 mL
4 tbsp.	softened butter	60 mL
2 tsp.	dry English-style mustard	10 mL
1 tsp.	Worcestershire sauce	5 mL
pinch	cayenne pepper	pinch
	salt to taste	
	paprika to taste	
1	1 lb. (500 g) loaf hearty whole grain bread or crusty rye bread, cut into 1 inch (2.5 cm) cubes, each cube including one edge of crust; air-dried 2 hours	1

Heat the ale or beer to a simmer over medium-low heat. Toss together the grated cheese and cornstarch. Add the cheese, in large handfuls, to the simmering liquid to melt. When the fondue is creamy and smooth, combine the butter, dry mustard, and Worcestershire and add to the fondue. Stir constantly with a wooden spoon until smooth and silky. Season with cayenne and a bit of salt (if needed), and place over a table-top burner. Keep the fondue at a gentle simmer. Sprinkle the top with a bit of paprika for colour.

Provide long fondue forks or bamboo skewers, so that guests may spear cubes of bread to swirl into the cheese fondue.

The Easy Gourmet features a photograph of this recipe on page 125.

SWISS CHOCOLATE FONDUE

No chocolate lover of any age can resist this easy—and sublime—warm chocolate fondue. Line a flat basket with crisp leaves and present the fondue surrounded by fresh seasonal fruits and cubes of pound cake.

4	3 oz. (90 g) Swiss milk chocolate bars, coarsely chopped	4
1/2 cup	whipping cream	125 mL
3 tbsp.	orange-flavoured liqueur, such as Cointreau, Grand Marnier, or Triple Sec (optional)	45 mL
2 pints	fresh strawberries, stems attached, rinsed and dried	1 L
1	fresh pineapple, stemmed, peeled, and cut in spears or wedges	1
2	apples, cut in wedges	2
2	pears, cut in chunks	2
	small clusters of grapes	
2-3 cups	pound cake, cut in cubes	500-750 mL

In a deep, heavy saucepan, melt the chopped chocolate and heat with the cream over low heat. Stir gently until the mixture is smooth. Add the liqueur.

Transfer the fondue to a warm fondue dish or heated bowl. Place over a small burner, if desired. Serve at once with the fruit and cake, and several bamboo skewers for each guest to use for dipping.

The Easy Gourmet features a photograph of this recipe on page 125.

A FTER-THEATRE DESSERT PARTY

After an evening of theatre or music, nothing satisfies like a selection of luscious light desserts, all served up with your fanciest china and glassware. Your dressed-up guests provide the backdrop and the conversation, and you provide the soft music and the perfect finishing-touch dessert buffet. Serves 8.

Icy Lemon Soufflé   *Chilled champagne*
Raspberry Poached Pears   *Assorted cookies (homemade or*
                                                  from the bakery)

ICY LEMON SOUFFLÉ

This light, refreshing lemon mousse looks spectacular rising from its pretty dish, garnished with thin lemon slices and fresh mint leaves. Serve icy cold.

6	eggs, separated	6
2 tbsp.	cornstarch	30 mL
1 1/4 cups	berry sugar	300 mL
2	envelopes unflavoured gelatin	2
1 1/2 cups	cold water	375 mL
1/2 cup	fresh lemon juice	125 mL
1 tbsp.	finely grated lemon rind (yellow part only)	15 mL
1 cup	whipping cream, chilled	250 mL
1/2 cup	finely chopped pistachios	125 mL
	lemon slices and fresh mint leaves for garnish	

In a heavy saucepan, whisk the egg yolks, cornstarch, 1 cup (250 mL) of the sugar and the gelatin until smooth. Whisk in the water and lemon juice until smooth. Heat over low heat, stirring, until the mixture coats the back of a spoon. Remove from the heat, transfer to a bowl, and stir in the lemon rind. Cool, and then chill 30-40 minutes, stirring several times, until the mixture begins to mound and thicken. Do not allow to set firm.

Prepare a 1 1/2 quart (1.5 L) soufflé dish by folding a long strip of waxed paper into thirds, 4 inches (10 cm) wide and long enough to wrap around the top of the dish with a slight overlap. Tie or tape the strip around the outside of the dish, extending 3 inches (7.5 cm) above the top edge. Set aside.

Beat the chilled cream until peaks form (do not whip dry). Beat the egg whites until soft peaks form. Add the remaining 1/4 cup (50 mL) sugar, and beat until stiff, glossy, meringue-like peaks form. Fold a spoonful of the egg whites into the chilled lemon mixture to loosen. Fold in the remaining egg whites, incorporating gently but thoroughly. Fold in the whipped cream. Pour the mixture into the prepared soufflé dish, so that it rises above the top edge of the dish but stays within the waxed paper collar. Chill the soufflé overnight to firm completely.

To serve, carefully peel off the waxed paper and discard. With a small spatula, press the pistachios into the sides of the soufflé. Decorate the top with thin slices of lemon and fresh mint leaves. Serve icy cold.

The Easy Gourmet features a photograph of this recipe on page 143.

RASPBERRY POACHED PEARS

Serve this sweet, refreshing dessert chilled, in your prettiest stemmed glass compote dish, with the lovely rosy syrup and a sprinkling of toasted slivered almonds or chopped pistachios.

2	15 oz. (425 g) pkgs. frozen sweetened raspberries, thawed, undrained	2
4 tbsp.	*each* fresh lemon and orange juice	60 mL
8	firm, ripe Bosc or Anjou pears, stems intact	8
1/2 cup	toasted slivered almonds or chopped pistachios (toast nuts in a 325°F (160°C) oven 8 minutes and cool)	125 mL
	fresh leaves or sprigs of mint for garnish (optional)	

Purée the berries, with their juice, and strain to remove seeds. Stir in the lemon and orange juices. Carefully peel each pear, leaving the stem intact. Slice a razor-thin slice off the bottom of each pear, so that they will stand upright. Place the pears in a large saucepan and cover with the raspberry sauce. Bring the liquid to a simmer. Swirl the pears to coat, cover, and poach over medium-low heat until tender, 10-12 minutes. Lift the pears from the syrup. Cool and chill.

Cook the remaining raspberry syrup over medium heat until thickened and reduced, about 10 minutes. Cool and chill.

To serve, place in a stemmed glass compote dish or in individual glass dishes. Spoon some of the chilled raspberry sauce over each pear. Top with a generous sprinkling of toasted nuts and garnish, if desired, with a pretty green mint leaf or sprig. Serve chilled.

The Easy Gourmet features a photograph of this recipe on page 143.

MIDNIGHT SPECIAL

There is something festive about a midnight meal, even on an ordinary day of the year. This menu is elegant enough for any holiday celebration and simple enough for a Saturday night. Make everything the day before—late-night entertaining was never this easy, or this luxurious! Serves 8.

Cream of Prawn Soup
Smoked Salmon Roulade
Individual Crême Brulée

CREAM OF PRAWN SOUP

Select large prawns with their shells on for this dish. Rich and creamy, it can be made ahead and gently reheated at serving time. Save a few perfect prawns for garnish.

1 lb.	large prawns in the shell	500 g
3/4 cup	butter	175 mL
2 cups	chopped onion	500 mL
1 cup	chopped celery	250 mL
1 tbsp.	chopped garlic	15 mL
1/2 cup	all-purpose flour	125 mL
3 cups	chicken stock	750 mL
3 tbsp.	tomato paste	45 mL
dash	bottled hot pepper sauce	dash

Peel the prawns and place the shells in a large pot. Cover with water and bring to a boil. Boil vigorously 20 minutes. Strain the liquid into a bowl and discard the shells, reserving the liquid.

In a large pot, melt the butter and add the onions, celery, and garlic. Sauté over medium-low heat until tender. Sprinkle on the flour and stir well. Add the chicken stock, reserved prawn stock and tomato paste. Bring to a boil, reduce the heat, and simmer 10 minutes. Cool slightly. Purée in a blender until smooth and thickened.

Clean the pot and return the soup to it. Reheat to simmering. Add the prawns and cook until they turn pink, about 5 minutes. Add hot pepper sauce to taste.

SMOKED SALMON ROULADE

A thin, savoury jelly roll is wrapped around a smooth cheese and smoked salmon filling in this made-for-a-party dish. Serve several slices to each guest on a chilled leaf of butter lettuce with Dilled Sour Cream alongside.

4 tbsp.	fine dry bread crumbs	60 mL
2 tbsp.	butter	30 mL
2 tbsp.	all-purpose flour	30 mL
1 cup	milk	250 mL
1 tsp.	mixed dry herbs such as savoury, chives, and basil	5 mL
1/2 tsp	salt	2 mL
1/2 tsp.	dry mustard	2 mL
dash	freshly ground black pepper	dash
8	eggs, separated	8
1/2 cup	grated Parmesan cheese	125 mL
	butter lettuce leaves	
	Smoked Salmon Filling (recipe follows)	
	Dilled Sour Cream (recipe follows)	

Grease a 15 x 10 x 3/4 inch (38 x 25 x 2 cm) jelly roll pan, line with parchment paper, and grease again. Sprinkle with the bread crumbs.

In a medium saucepan, melt the butter and stir in the flour. Cook 2-3 minutes. Whisk in the milk and cook until the mixture is smooth and comes to a boil. Whisk in the herbs and seasonings.

Beat the egg yolks lightly and whisk in a little of the hot milk mixture to warm them up. Return the egg mixture to the sauce, whisking constantly. Cook 1 minute longer. Stir in 4 tbsp. (60 mL) of the cheese. Cool.

Heat the oven to 400°F (200°C). Beat the egg whites until stiff but not dry. Stir 1/4 of the beaten egg whites into the cooled yolk mixture to lighten, then fold in the remaining egg whites gently but thoroughly. Spread evenly in the prepared pan and bake 20 minutes or until golden and firm to the touch.

When the roll is done, remove from the oven and sprinkle with the remaining cheese. Cover with a piece of waxed paper or parchment, then a clean tea towel, and invert onto a work surface. Carefully remove the parchment from the bottom. Trim off the crusty edges. Spread with Smoked Salmon Filling and gently roll up from the long side. Refrigerate, seam side down, for a few hours. When ready to serve, cut into 1 inch (2.5 cm) rounds. Serve on leaves of butter lettuce, accompanied by a bowl of Dilled Sour Cream.

SMOKED SALMON FILLING

1	8 oz. (250 g) pkg. cream cheese	1
1/4 lb.	smoked salmon, diced	125 g
4 tbsp.	sour cream	60 mL
2 tbsp.	fresh lemon juice	30 mL
2	green onions, chopped	2

Blend all the ingredients together in a food processor or blender until the mixture reaches a spreading consistency.

DILLED SOUR CREAM

1 cup	sour cream	250 mL
1 tbsp.	chopped fresh dill, or	15 mL
1 tsp.	dried dill	5 mL

Blend all the ingredients together and serve in a small bowl alongside the Smoked Salmon Roulade.

INDIVIDUAL CRÊME BRULÉE

This is a baked custard with a crispy brown sugar crust, a truly elegant dessert. Make the custard a day or two ahead of time, top with the brown sugar, and run it under the broiler just before serving.

3 cups	whipping cream	750 mL
1	vanilla bean, or	1
1 tbsp.	vanilla	15 mL
5	egg yolks	5
4 tbsp.	sugar	60 mL
	brown sugar for garnish	

Put 8 custard cups, ramekins, or small ceramic bowls in a large pan. Pour hot water into the pan until it reaches halfway up the sides of the dishes. Set aside.

Place the cream and vanilla bean in a medium saucepan and heat to scalding (tiny bubbles will form around the edges). Remove from the heat and remove the vanilla bean.

Meanwhile, beat the egg yolks and sugar until the sugar is dissolved and the mixture is very thick. Add the hot cream in a slow, steady stream, beating constantly. (If you are using vanilla extract, add it at this point). Pour carefully into the baking dishes.

Heat the oven to 325°F (160°C). Butter pieces of parchment or waxed paper to fit the tops of the baking dishes and place over the custard, to prevent a skin from forming. Bake 60-70 minutes or until a knife inserted slightly off centre comes out clean. Remove from the oven and lift the dishes from the pan of water. Refrigerate until very cold. Remove the parchment lids.

When ready to serve, place the custard cups on a baking sheet. Sprinkle the tops with a thin layer of brown sugar. Broil until the sugar is melted and medium brown. Watch carefully—this only takes a few minutes. Serve at once.

Note: While a vanilla bean may seem expensive, it can be used several times. The fresh bean is best when split down the centre. After using, pat it dry and replace it in its tube. When it has been used 2 or 3 times, tuck it in a small bowl of sugar to make vanilla sugar for your tea or coffee.

CHOCOLATE LOVERS' DELIGHT

If your guests aren't confirmed chocoholics already, they will be after they join you at this wickedly good dessert mini-buffet. Use the best chocolate you can get, put out some brightly coloured linens and shiny cutlery, and take turns swooning! Serves 8.

Chocolate Bread Pudding
Pecan Pie with Chocolate
   Mousse

Deluxe chocolate ice cream
Chilled whipped cream
Bowls of shaved chocolate for
   garnish

CHOCOLATE BREAD PUDDING

Here is an old favourite, updated with chocolate and a quick custard. Served warm from the oven with the cold custard spooned on top, this is comfort food at its best. Serves 8.

1 qt.	warmed milk	1 L
5	eggs	5
2 cups	sugar	500 mL
1 tsp.	vanilla	5 mL
4 oz.	chocolate, melted and cooled	125 g
15	slices French bread, crusts removed	15

In a large bowl, beat together the milk, eggs, sugar, and vanilla. Beat in the cooled chocolate. Break the bread into bite-sized pieces and add. Press down and let stand until the bread has absorbed most of the mixture. The dish may be made ahead to this point.

Heat the oven to 375°F (190°C). Grease a 10 inch (25 cm) square baking pan and pour in the mixture. Bake 50-60 minutes or until puffed and set. Serve warm. The pudding reheats well.

Opposite: After-Theatre Dessert Party (pp. 136-37) and selections from Chocolate Lovers' Delight (pp. 142-46)—(top to bottom) Icy Lemon Soufflé, Pecan Pie with Chocolate Mousse, Raspberry Poached Pears.

Custard

2 tbsp.	*each* cornstarch and all-purpose flour	30 mL
1/2 cup	sugar	125 mL
3	egg yolks, beaten	3
2 1/2 cups	milk	625 mL

In a small bowl, mix together the cornstarch, flour, and sugar. Set aside. In another small bowl, beat the egg yolks. Set aside.

In a medium saucepan, bring the milk to a rolling boil and pour half of it over the cornstarch mixture. Whisk well. Whisk in the egg yolks. Return the remaining milk to the heat and bring to a rolling boil again. Pour into the cornstarch-egg mixture, whisking. The custard should have thickened. If not, return it to the heat and cook for 1-2 minutes. Place plastic wrap right on the warm surface of the custard to prevent a skin from forming. It will thicken upon standing. Serve cold.

PECAN PIE WITH CHOCOLATE MOUSSE

A luscious, creamy mousse tops a rich pecan-filled pie in this truly decadent concoction. Serve only to dessert lovers!

1	4 oz. (125 g) pkg. cream cheese	1
2 tbsp.	sugar	30 mL
2 tsp.	vanilla	10 mL
1	unbaked 10 inch (25 cm) pie shell	1
3 oz.	whole pecans, toasted	90 g
3	eggs	3
3/4 cup	light corn syrup	175 mL
2 tbsp.	sugar	30 mL
Chocolate Mousse (recipe follows)		
whipped cream, pecans, and chocolate curls for garnish		

Combine the cream cheese, sugar, and 1 tsp. (5 mL) of the vanilla in a bowl and mix until smooth. Spead over the bottom of the pie shell in a pie pan or quiche dish. Press the pecans into the cheese mixture.

In another bowl, beat the eggs, corn syrup, sugar and remaining 1 tsp. (5 mL) vanilla until well mixed. Gently pour over the pecans.

Heat the oven to 400°F (200°C) and bake 30-35 minutes or until the crust is browned and the top is puffy and golden. Cool and chill.

Spread the Chocolate Mousse generously over top. Chill until set, about 4 hours. At serving time, garnish with swirls of whipped cream, then sprinkle on pecans and chocolate curls.

CHOCOLATE MOUSSE

4 oz.	semi-sweet chocolate, melted and cooled	125 g
3	eggs, separated	3
1 tbsp.	water	15 mL
1 cup	whipping cream	250 mL
4 tbsp.	icing sugar	60 mL

Place the cooled chocolate into a medium bowl. Beat the egg yolks and water until thick and lemon-coloured. Blend into the chocolate.

In another bowl, beat the cream until soft peaks form. Beat in 2 tbsp. (30 mL) of the icing sugar. Fold into the chocolate mixture.

Beat the egg whites until soft peaks form. Beat in the remaining 2 tbsp. (30 mL) icing sugar. Fold into the chocolate mixture. Spoon over the cold pecan pie. Chill until set.

The Easy Gourmet features a photograph of this recipe on page 143.

AUTUMN BONFIRE PARTY

Fireworks, bonfires, the cold nip of autumn air—these are the stuff of late autumn memories. This grand outdoor feast, loaded with the fragrances and flavours of the fall harvest, is guaranteed to warm the toes, and the hearts, of your guests. Serves 8.

Pumpkin Soup
Build-Your-Own Stuffed
  Potatoes
Caramel Candy Apples

Hot spiced apple punch
Assorted cookies (homemade or
  from the bakery)

PUMPKIN SOUP

Served hot with a hint of spice, this smooth, rich soup sets the mood for fireworks and bonfires! Serve either in one large, hollowed-out pumpkin shell, or in small individual pumpkin shells.

2	14 oz. (398 mL) cans pumpkin	2
4 cups	chicken stock	1 L
2 tsp.	instant minced onion	10 mL
1/2 tsp.	ground ginger	2 mL
1/2 tsp.	ground nutmeg	2 mL
1 tsp.	salt	5 mL
2 cups	half-and-half cream	500 mL
	chopped fresh parsley for garnish	

Blend together the pumpkin, chicken stock, onion, ginger, nutmeg, and salt in a large microproof casserole. Cover and microwave on HIGH 100% power to bring to a boil, stirring once during the cooking time.

Reduce the power level to MEDIUM LOW 30%, cover, and microwave 10 minutes, stirring halfway through the cooking time.

Blend in the cream. Return to the microwave and cook on MEDIUM 50% power until heated through.

Serve in a hollowed-out pumpkin shell, sprinkled with chopped fresh parsley.

BUILD-YOUR-OWN STUFFED POTATOES

Baked potatoes are a tradition at bonfire parties. Update that tradition and use your microwave to bake the potatoes. Serve them with a choice of tempting toppings, all of which can be prepared ahead and reheated in the microwave at serving time.

MICROWAVE-BAKED POTATOES

Select medium potatoes about the same size and shape and you have the start of a delicious, nutritious meal-in-a-dish. Offer several toppings.

8	medium potatoes	8

Scrub the potatoes well and vent by cutting a cross through the skin on the top of each potato. Arrange them "bicycle spoke" fashion in a circle in the microwave. Microwave on HIGH 100% power, allowing 5-7 minutes per medium potato. Halfway through the cooking time, turn each potato over and turn sideways 180°.

When cooked, open each potato by pushing through the cross-cut vent. Wrap each potato in foil to keep warm for serving.

BROCCOLI CHEESE TOPPING

1 lb.	fresh or frozen broccoli florets	500 g
4 tbsp.	all-purpose flour	60 mL
1 tsp.	salt	5 mL
1/2 tsp.	white pepper	2 mL
1/2 tsp.	dry mustard	2 mL
4 tbsp.	butter	60 mL
2 cups	milk	500 mL
2 cups	grated cheddar cheese	500 mL
4 tbsp.	grated Parmesan cheese	60 mL
	grated Parmesan cheese for garnish	

Place the broccoli in a microproof bowl. Cover and microwave on HIGH 100% power until cooked, stirring halfway through the cooking time. Let stand, covered. Mix together the flour, salt, pepper, and dry mustard. Set aside.

In an 8 cup (2 L) microproof dish, melt the butter on HIGH 100% power 1-1 1/2 minutes until bubbling. Blend in the flour mixture. Gradually blend in the milk. Return to the microwave and cook on HIGH 100% power in 2 minute increments, stirring well after each cooking period, until the mixture comes to a full boil. Microwave on HIGH 100% power 1 minute longer. Stir in the cheeses. Return to the microwave and cook on MEDIUM 50% power 1-2 minutes, if necessary, to melt the cheeses. Stir in the cooked broccoli.

Serve with extra grated Parmesan cheese for topping.

CHILI BEEF TOPPING

1 lb.	ground beef	500 g
1 tbsp.	chili powder	15 mL
1 tsp.	salt	5 mL
dash	hot chili sauce	dash
2	15 oz. (425 g) cans chili con carne with beans	2
2 cups	grated cheddar cheese	500 mL

Place the ground beef in a microproof bowl. Microwave on MEDIUM 50% power until cooked, stirring twice during the cooking time. Crumble the meat and drain off excess fat. Stir in the chili powder, salt, and chili sauce. Microwave on MEDIUM 50% power for 2 minutes. Stir in the chili con carne. Microwave on MEDIUM 50% power 4-6 minutes until heated through, stirring during the cooking time.

Serve with the grated cheese for topping.

SPICY TOMATO CHICKEN TOPPING

1 lb.	chicken pieces	500 g
2	14 oz. (398 mL) cans Mexican tomato sauce	2
1 tsp.	celery salt	5 mL
1/2 tsp.	cayenne pepper	2 mL
2 tbsp.	hot taco sauce	30 mL
dash	bottled hot pepper sauce	dash
2 cups	finely shredded lettuce	500 mL

Place the chicken pieces in a microproof dish, with the thicker portions towards the outside edge of the dish. Cover with waxed paper and microwave on MEDIUM HIGH 70% power, allowing 6-8 minutes per pound (500 g). Allow to cool, covered. Discard the skin and bones and cut into 1/2 inch (1 cm) cubes.

Mix together the remaining ingredients, except for the lettuce. Pour over the cubed chicken, cover, and microwave on MEDIUM 50% power until the sauce is heated through.

Serve with shredded lettuce for topping.

FRUITY CURRIED LAMB TOPPING

2	10 oz. (284 mL) cans curry sauce	2
1/2 cup	raisins	125 mL
1/2 cup	dried apricots, diced	125 mL
1/2 cup	pitted prunes, diced	125 mL
1	apple, peeled and chopped	1
1 tbsp.	curry powder	15 mL
2 cups	diced cooked lamb	500 mL
4 tbsp.	shredded coconut	60 mL
1 cup	mango chutney	250 mL

Place the curry sauce, raisins, apricots, prunes, apple, and curry powder in a microproof dish. Cover and microwave on HIGH 100% power 3-5 minutes until the apple is soft, stirring at least once during the cooking time.

Stir in the lamb and coconut. Microwave on MEDIUM 50% power 5-7 minutes until the lamb is heated through.

Serve with the mango chutney for topping.

SOUR CREAM, BACON AND ONION TOPPING

1 cup	chopped onion	250 mL
1/2 lb.	bacon, chopped	250 g
2 cups	sour cream	500 mL
1 tsp.	seasoning salt	5 mL
1 tsp.	black pepper	5 mL
1 cup	peeled, seeded, and chopped tomato	250 mL

Place the onion and bacon in a microproof dish. Cover and microwave on HIGH 100% power 4-6 minutes until the onion is soft and the bacon is cooked, stirring at least once during the cooking time. Drain off excess fat. Stir in the sour cream, salt, and pepper. Microwave on MEDIUM LOW 30% power until the sour cream is heated through, stirring during the cooking time. Serve warm with the chopped tomato for topping.

CARAMEL CANDY APPLES

A perennial favourite, these treats will be in instant demand for dessert, by young and old alike.

2 tbsp.	butter	30 mL
12	medium apples	12
12	wooden popsicle sticks	12
2 lbs.	caramels	1 kg
4 tbsp.	water	60 mL
1/2 tsp.	ground cinnamon	2 mL

Generously butter a large microproof casserole dish, as well as a piece of waxed paper cut to line a cookie sheet. Push a wooden popsicle stick through the stalk end of each apple. Unwrap the caramels. Place them with the water in the casserole dish. Microwave on MEDIUM HIGH 70% power 4 minutes. Stir well and microwave on MEDIUM HIGH 70% power until the caramels are melted. Blend in the cinnamon. Dip each apple in caramel, turning to coat evenly. Stand on buttered waxed paper until set. If the caramel thickens as you work, cover the dish and return it to the microwave on MEDIUM HIGH 70% power to soften. Stir well before using.

DESSERT LOVERS' SMORGASBORD

Here is a selection of desserts that will satisfy even the sweetest sweet tooth. Serve it late in the evening, after a good round of night life with friends, among shining china and crystal and plenty of candlelight. Serves 6-8.

Caramelized Lime Cheesecake
Fresh Lemon and Ginger Pie
Cappuccino Mandarin Pavlova

CARAMELIZED LIME CHEESECAKE

Here are two desserts in one—the creamy smoothness of cheesecake and the rich, amber-coloured sauce of a crème caramel. Serve it with generous portions of colourful fresh sliced fruits.

1	8 oz. (250 g) pkg. cream cheese, at room temperature	1
6	eggs	6
1/2 cup	sugar	125 mL
2 cups	milk	500 mL
1/2 tsp.	vanilla	2 mL
2 tsp.	grated lime rind	10 mL

Caramel Topping

3/4 cup	sugar	175 mL
	fresh sliced strawberries and sliced kiwi fruit	
	for decoration	
	whipped cream (optional)	

Heat the oven to 350°F (180°C).

Place the cream cheese in a large mixing bowl and cut into small pieces. Beat with an electric mixer until smooth. In a separate bowl, beat the eggs and the 1/2 cup (125 mL) sugar until well blended. Gradually beat into the cream cheese until smooth.

In a small saucepan, heat the milk but do not boil. Pour into the cream cheese mixture gradually, beating until smooth. Stir in the vanilla and lime rind. Set aside.

To make the caramel topping, in a heavy-based skillet, heat the 3/4 cup (175 mL) sugar over medium-low heat, stirring occasionally, until dissolved and golden brown, about 10 minutes. Watch it carefully so it does not burn. Pour quickly and carefully (the mixture is very hot) into the bottom of an 8 inch (20 cm) round cake pan with 2 inch (5 cm) sides. Pour the cream cheese mixture on top. Place the pan in a roasting pan and add water to the roasting pan to a depth of 1/2 inch (1 cm).

Bake 50-60 minutes until set. Lift the cake pan out of the roasting pan and let cool completely in the refrigerator for several hours.

Just before serving, turn out the cake onto a round plate with sides. Decorate the top and sides with the strawberries and kiwi fruit. Serve with whipped cream if desired.

FRESH LEMON AND GINGER PIE

The tang of lemon blended with the mystical scent of ginger makes this creamy, fresh-tasting dessert unique. It is a very deep pie, so make sure to use a deep pie dish.

1/3 cup	butter or margarine	75 mL
1 1/2 cups	ginger snap cookie crumbs	375 mL
	(about 24 cookies, crushed)	
1 cup	whipping cream	250 mL
1/2 cup	fresh lemon juice	125 mL
1 1/2 tsp.	grated lemon rind	7 mL
1	envelope unflavoured gelatin	1
4 tbsp.	cold water	60 mL
1	8 oz. (250 g) pkg. cream cheese,	1
	at room temperature	
1	10 1/2 oz. (300 mL) can sweetened condensed milk	1
1/3 cup	finely chopped preserved ginger, drained	75 mL
1/2 cup	sour cream	125 mL
	fresh blueberries (or frozen and thawed)	
	for decoration	

In a small saucepan, melt the butter. Stir in the cookie crumbs and press into a deep 9 inch (23 cm) pie plate.

Pour the cream into a large mixing bowl and stir in the lemon juice and rind. Let stand in the refrigerator 10 minutes.

In a small bowl, combine the gelatin with the cold water. Set over a pan of simmering water and stir until the gelatin has dissolved. Remove from the water and set aside. In another large bowl, beat the cream cheese with an electric mixer until smooth. Gradually beat in the condensed milk until smooth.

Beat the cream mixture until it just begins to stiffen. Pour it into the cream cheese mixture, beating until smooth and well blended. Pour in the gelatin in a thin, steady stream. Stir in the ginger. Pour this mixture into the pie crust. (It will be very full.) Chill for at least 2 hours until firm.

Just before serving, beat the sour cream until smooth and spread over the top of the pie. Pile the blueberries in the middle.

CAPPUCCINO MANDARIN PAVLOVA

The distinctive taste of espresso coffee gives a unique flavour to this delightful dessert. Buy an espresso coffee "to go" from the deli department, or use instant espresso coffee.

Pavlova

3	egg whites	3
2 tsp.	instant coffee powder	10 mL
1 tsp.	cornstarch	5 mL
1 tsp.	white vinegar	5 mL
1 tsp.	cold water	5 mL
1 cup	sugar	250 mL

Cappuccino Cream

3 tbsp.	cornstarch	45 mL
3 tbsp.	sugar	45 mL
2/3 cup	milk	150 mL
1/3 cup	espresso coffee	75 mL
3	egg yolks, beaten	3
1 cup	whipping cream	250 mL
1	10 oz. (284 mL) can mandarin oranges, drained on paper towels	1

Heat the oven to 300°F (150°C). Line a cookie sheet with foil.

To make the Pavlova, in a large bowl, whisk the egg whites until stiff. In a small bowl, mix together the coffee powder, cornstarch, vinegar, and water until the coffee is dissolved. Gradually whisk the sugar into the egg whites, then mix in the coffee mixture just until well combined.

Spread the mixture on the cookie sheet into an 8 inch (20 cm) circle, about 1 inch (2.5 cm) thick. (Or spread the Pavlova on a 9-10 inch (23-25 cm) flat ovenproof serving plate, so the pavlova can be served as well as baked on it.) Place in the oven, and immediately reduce the heat to 275°F (140°C). Bake 1 hour, or until the Pavlova is crisp on the outside and marshmallow-like inside. Cool completely on the cookie sheet. It will look cracked.

To make the cappuccino cream, in a small saucepan, blend together the cornstarch and sugar. Gradually stir in the milk and coffee. Cook over high heat, stirring constantly, until the mixture boils and thickens. Remove from the heat and beat in the egg yolks. Return to medium heat and cook, stirring, for 1 minute, to cook the egg yolks. Cover with a piece of waxed paper to prevent a skin from forming and place in the refrigerator until completely chilled.

To serve, whisk the coffee mixture until smooth. Whip the cream until stiff and fold it into the coffee mixture. Carefully peel the foil from underneath the Pavlova and place on a flat serving plate. Spoon the cappuccino cream on top and pile the oranges over it. Serve immediately.

INDEX